No Death

No Death
God's Other Door

Hugh Lynn Cayce
and Edgar Cayce

Compiled and edited by
Graham L. McGill

ARE
PRESS

**ASSOCIATION FOR
RESEARCH AND
ENLIGHTENMENT**

A.R.E. Press • Virginia Beach • Virginia

A.R.E. Press
215 67th Street
Virginia Beach, VA 23451-2061

Library of Congress Cataloging-in-Publication Data
Cayce, Hugh Lynn.
   No death , God's other door / Hugh Lynn Cayce and Edgar
Cayce; compiled and edited by Graham L. McGill
      p.   cm.
   ISBN 0-87604-417-8 (trade paper)
   1. Death. 2. Future life. 3. Cayce, Edgar, 1877-1945.
I. McGill, Graham L., 1933- . II. Title.
BF1311.F8C39   1998
133.9'01'3—DC21   98-37645

Cover design by Lightbourne Images

Contents

Preface

In the late '50s, when *God's Other Door* was first written, Hugh Lynn Cayce didn't have much time for literary work. He was on the road constantly, speaking in every state on any Cayce topic. The Association for Research and Enlightenment, Inc. (A.R.E.), which Hugh Lynn was trying to build and keep alive more than ten years after his father's death, consisted of only a few thousand members. Yet he created a short, classic book on death and the realms beyond death.

To revise and enlarge such a book using other materials by Hugh Lynn was a tremendous challenge, I realized. For the first several weeks I gathered related materials—reading transcriptions from A.R.E. Press, transcribing stories from audiotapes, and taking notes from other Hugh Lynn Cayce books. But when I actually started putting down words, I ran into a stumbling block.

I found myself hanging back, feeling uncertain, daunted, overwhelmed. I was asking myself, "Would Hugh Lynn use this word, or that?" "How can I add transitional material but keep from putting words in Hugh Lynn's mouth?" "How can I manage a revision, yet remain consistent with Hugh Lynn's original version?" I seemed to be constantly scratching my head, biting my lip, and fetching coffee.

After all, I had not grown up as Edgar Cayce's son. My encounter with the Cayce material was my own, not Hugh Lynn's. I had spent my adult life as a newspaper editor, not as A.R.E. administrator or lecturer on the world of the psyche.

As head of the A.R.E., Hugh Lynn had been an imposing figure to me; at times, he even seemed forbidding and stern. Yet I knew that many A.R.E. members revered him greatly, still spoke lovingly of him. Painfully, I began to wonder if I had bitten off more than I could chew.

Then I had a dream.

Hugh Lynn had been sitting at a table with me, laughing and chatting. Carefree and jaunty in short-sleeves, he'd been tilting back in his chair, chortling and gesturing. He agreed with me that *God's Other Door* needed revising. He was sure, he said, that I was "the guy" to do it. He hadn't had a computer when he wrote it in 1958, he said, let alone a CD-ROM, and he thought I could add many readings he hadn't had time to locate at the outset. He'd be there to help when I needed him, he assured me. To confirm his belief in my ability, he gave me "his secret code number" to the whole A.R.E. computer system, which, I told myself in the dream, as a matter of honor, I would not remember. And, thinking about it later that morning, I found I could not!

Grinning as I awoke, I felt as if I'd just received a pat on the back from the Beyond. "Thank you, Hugh Lynn, for showing up in my dream," I said.

Revising *God's Other Door* went easier after that.

Graham L. McGill

Introduction

Who Was Edgar Cayce?

The "sleeping" Edgar Cayce was a medical diagnostician. During his life (1877-1945) he helped thousands with diseases ranging from boils to insanity. Many believe that he either saved or changed their lives when all seemed lost. He is still helping people today with the over 14,000 readings preserved and distributed by the Association for Research and Enlightenment, Inc. (A.R.E.).

Many books have told this story—*There Is a River, Many Mansions,* and *The Sleeping Prophet*—to mention a few. The "sleeping" Cayce is well known through these books. I, his son, will tell of the Edgar Cayce I knew while he was awake.

Outwardly, at times, he could seem rather ordinary. He enjoyed catching perch in a Kentucky pond and sail-fishing off the Florida coast. He liked games—checkers, bowling, croquet, golf—though he was one of the worst golfers I've ever seen.

He was a man of many skills.

As a photographer in those days, he not only took pictures, but developed, printed, mounted, and framed them. Mom helped in this business by hand-painting some of the early ones. He sometimes used Mom and me as models for his photos. Parents brought children to him from all over Alabama, and he eventually became known as a fine photographer of children. His picture of a cotton plant in bloom won many prizes.

Wherever we lived, Dad had a workshop. He could mend anything. He was a good carpenter. When we were old enough, he taught my brother and me to work with tools (an accomplishment in itself). The family was always adding to or remodeling the house—painting, concreting, making walls with lath and plaster. He'd grown up on a farm, you know, and never completely forgot the skills he acquired there. He was proud of his gardens—the variety of trees in our yard, and the berry bushes he cultivated with care and devotion.

He also made preserves, jellies, and wines, often in large quantities. During Prohibition, he was investigated, not as a psychic, but as a potential moonshiner, because he bought such large quantities of sugar! Sometimes Mom would go to Hopkinsville to visit kinfolk and return to a pantry crammed with brandied peaches, jellies, figs, and vats of wines. During his life he gave away thousands of jars of preserves.

As we grew up, my brother and I were encouraged to

bring friends home. Mother always had something for them to eat, and Dad was easy and sociable with people of all ages. After our move to Virginia Beach, he encouraged me to help out with the local Boy Scout troop.

We built a Scout cabin on Linkhorn Bay, a then-undeveloped wooded area. One Scout father could drill wells, but couldn't find anything but brackish water. When I mentioned this to Dad, he insisted we go right over. On the way he cut a peach branch in the shape of a "Y." At the cabin site he held the "Y" in front of his chest and walked back and forth until the pointer turned down. Finally, he drove a stake and told me we'd get good water at thirty-two feet. The well driller dug and got good water at thirty-two and a half feet. Dad, it seems, was also a dowser.

He spent some time every day during good weather fishing for perch in the little lake in back of our house. He built a pier into the water and put a comfortable seat on the end of it. He planted a small willow tree in a tar-lined box filled with soil, and attached a rope so that he could pull the floating tree out to shade him on hot days.

Encouraged by Dad and Mom, my brother and I had many pets while we were growing up. These included dogs—a whole series of them—all of whom loved my father; also rabbits, canaries, goldfish, and a parrot. The parrot loved to sit on Dad's shoulder and gently touch his ear. We had all seen this bird crush a lead pencil with his sharp beak and so watched this in awe. I say "his" sharp beak, but during his last days with us, "he" built a nest out of newspaper shreds and laid an egg, thereafter becoming "Miss Polly."

Dad was a great storyteller. My brother and I especially loved his stories about the fierce sheepdog he had had back on the farm in Hopkinsville, Kentucky. According to him, the sheepdog once fought and killed several other dogs who'd attacked his sheep.

Money was often a concern in our family. There was either too little (long periods) or too much (short periods). Sometimes Dad spent money as if his supply were inexhaustible. Then he'd fret about it. He'd buy jars, fruit, and sugar for a big preserving spree, even if it left us without much to eat except bread and preserves. If he happened to see a good buy on a tree he wanted, the cupboard sometimes looked pretty bare for a while. But he was generous with his time and money—generous with his family, friends, and people he worked for.

He also had a quick temper, which he worked at controlling all his life. He suffered from extremes of emotion—very happy or very glum, very talkative or very silent, very optimistic or very pessimistic. He was often moody and sentimental. When he laughed, the world was light and breezy; when he frowned, the world was very dark. He trusted everyone and was often led astray by friends. He forgave others easily; he was harder on himself.

My father radiated concern and love. These attitudes showed in his desire to help people through his readings, his kindness to children, his thoughtfulness with servants. His patience with young people was important in his success with groups. When he traveled, he was soon on friendly terms with everyone he met. Dad never showed irritation with a waiter or waitress that I remember. All kinds of people were drawn to him.

Throughout his life, he kept up a full schedule of church activities—janitor of a little country church at age ten, later a Sunday school teacher, leader of Christian Endeavor societies, deacon, adult Bible class leader. In Hopkinsville, Louisville, Bowling Green, and Selma, he encouraged church members in their work with prisoners. He personally gave away many Bibles to prisoners. He was a popular Sunday school teacher; his class in Selma at one time was reported as being the largest in Alabama. During those years he belonged to the Disciples of Christ. When we moved to Virginia Beach, we joined the Presbyterian Church.

As far back as I can remember, Edgar Cayce read from his Bible every day. I remember, too, his constancy in prayer, his quiet times by himself. It could truly be said of him that he prayed "without ceasing." I think this was how he nurtured the illumination he had had, so that it remained a firm foundation for the more complex experiences that came later, experiences which kept his whole being in tune with the Infinite Benevolence he sought to serve.

Growing up as his son was a constant adventure. As a small boy, I began to realize that I could never kid my father, could never lie to him about anything.

I disobeyed my father once while we were living in Selma, Alabama. I went skinny-dipping with friends in the Alabama River. When I came home, he stopped me on the landing as I was rushing up the stairs.

"Where have you been?" he challenged.

I lied.

He scowled, squinted, shook his head, then proceeded to tell me exactly where I'd been—a new place we'd picked out that day—precisely what I'd been doing, how one boy had cut his foot and limped home bleeding.

That scared the daylights out of me.

Another time, I tried to get him to play bridge. I caught him just after lunch—he'd come in to rest for a few minutes. I was sitting at the bridge table and had dealt four bridge hands. I said, "Dad, why don't you like to play bridge? You play all these other games—pitch, rook, Parcheesi, 500—why don't you like bridge?"

He said, "Well, with bridge you have to concentrate so

hard it's easy to read your mind."

I said, "Oh, come on now. You're pretty good when you're asleep. But I haven't seen you do this kind of thing when you're awake. I can't imagine that you could read a bridge hand."

"Yeah?" And this made him mad—that I would doubt him. "Pick up that hand in front of you!" he ordered.

I tried to placate him, "Oh now, forget about it, it's all right, forget about it."

"Pick up that hand!"

I did, and he called all thirteen cards right across, got up, snorted, and said, "That's why I don't like to play bridge!" And he walked out.

I never asked him again.

Hugh Lynn Cayce

*Ode. Intimations of Immortality from
Recollections of Early Childhood*

"Our birth is but a sleep and a forgetting:
The soul that rises with us, our life's star,
Hath had elsewhere its setting,
And cometh from afar:
Not in entire forgetfulness,
And not in utter nakedness,
But trailing clouds of glory do we come
From God, who is our home . . . "

William Wordsworth

1

Out-of-Body Experiences

In 1927, when I was a freshman at Washington and Lee University, I was having trouble with a sophomore, Gus Elias. Gus was a bright intellectual who had taken upon himself the job of straightening us out—Tom Sugrue, my roommate, and me—of qualifying for us ignorant freshmen exactly what we ought to believe in. Gus was an agnostic, Tom a Catholic, and I was always telling stories about Edgar Cayce. Gus's view was that when you're dead, you're dead, and he was trying to straighten Tom out of his strong Catholic beliefs and straighten me out of anything psychic.

We went to the post office at noon one day after classes, picked up the mail, sat down on the post office steps, and argued for several hours, skipping lunch. Afterward, Gus went on to a dance at Natural Bridge, Virginia, a resort near Lexington. And Tom and I, as freshmen are supposed to do, went back to the dorm, studied, and went to bed.

While I was asleep, I had a strange experience. I found myself sitting up in bed, but my body was still lying down. I began to realize that I was having an out-of-body experience, able to move from the body, back and forth. I began to do that, simply by willing. I could slide out of and back into my body again. I'd been told that you had to go in through the mouth or one of the holes in your body. It is not so. You can go in from the top, or the bottom, or sideways. I came in and made a three-point landing, and came up through the mattress, and back into the body. I had this great sense of freedom—it was fascinating! This body was snoring away nicely on this bed. And suddenly, I was able to think myself onto the molding. I can close my eyes now and remember vividly the dust on that molding. It was amazing, the perception that I had.

Then, as I was moving around in the room—I didn't try to get far away from the body—the room began to fill up with a light cloud. It was absolutely dark in the room, but I could see easily because of the light from this cloud. My body was on the bed, but my consciousness moved to the floor in the middle of the room. It was not a large room, and it became crowded with that cloud in it. Suddenly, out of the cloud, came Gus Elias's hand, and voice, "Cayce, come up here. Come up here. This is terrific. I've got to show you!" The hand pulled back, and I moved, stood up to try to follow the hand, and to make contact with Gus. Everything was fuzzy, but I was trying to follow his suggestion. As I touched the cloud, it was cold. I became frightened. I snapped back into my body and woke up, really woke up this time, all of me, body and consciousness together. My body felt cold and clammy. I sat up and turned on the light.

It was two o'clock. I began to wonder what kind of crazy, cockeyed dream I'd had. Then somebody pounded on the door and said, "Cayce, get up, and get over to the hospital. They're bringing Gus Elias's body in. He was killed in an automobile accident around twelve o'clock. That's when the clocks on the car stopped when it crashed."

What had happened? Did I in that sensitive sleep state know all about Gus's death, and then somehow make contact? I will tell you what I think: Gus was continuing our debate! He was continuing to think and talk about what we'd been discussing all afternoon, and I got a demonstration that clinched the argument for me—when you're dead, you're *not* dead!

This happened a long time ago. I offer it merely as a personal experience, not as evidence, not proof of anything. I am not trying to convince you of anything. I couldn't explain it at the time, and I'm not sure I can now, but I've thought a lot about it, and I have some theories.

Similar stories are told by many.

Growing up as Edgar Cayce's son was like having a powerful microscope or telescope in your living room. It enabled perception of otherwise unsuspected objects. I became aware that the world is far more complex than most people believe or than is discernible through our five senses.

As I traveled across the country, talking about my experiences with my father, other people approached me to share their experiences. Here's an example:

After a lecture in Sacramento a woman came up and said, "I was here in California, and my daughter in Oregon had had a baby. I wanted to go and see this child. I had talked to her on the phone, and the baby had come, and everything was fine. I wanted to go, was planning on going, but hadn't done it yet.

"One night I was cooking supper, waiting for my husband to come home, and I went in and lay down on the bed—still had on my apron from the kitchen. I dropped off into a semiconscious state" (in between wakefulness and sleep; *hypnogogic,* they call it), "and suddenly I was standing in my daughter's home in Oregon. Her husband was home from work, and was holding and talking to the baby. Suddenly they both looked up and saw me standing in the door. They were very surprised. And their surprise, I guess, startled me back into my body, back to where I was in California.

"In a few minutes the phone rang. My daughter was wanting to know where I was—was I all right? They thought I was dead! They had seen me in Oregon! The funny part was—they didn't see me with my apron; they saw me in my best dress, the one I'd just bought and was planning to wear when I went to Oregon. It seemed I just put it on and went!"

I said, "Do you mean that both of these people saw you in Oregon while you were here in California?"

She said, "Yes. My daughter's right here. You can talk to her about it."

The daughter confirmed it. I said, "Do you mean your husband saw your mother, too?"

She said, "Yes."

"Can I talk to your husband?"

She said, "Yes." And I went right to the telephone and called him long distance.

I didn't tell him I knew anything, just asked him to tell the story. Without any prompting, he told me essentially what the mother and daughter had told me.

Another example: After a lecture in Pittsburgh, a man came up and said:

"Hugh Lynn, I've got a problem. Sometime ago, in the electrical shop where I was working, I grabbed a wrong wire and it burned me and knocked me out. Thinking I was dead, they rushed me to the hospital. But I didn't go to the hospital. I went home to my wife. I found her sitting at the table, talking to a neighbor, drinking a cup of coffee. I was there. I was standing right there looking at them. But apparently they couldn't see me. I heard the phone ring, I heard them being told that I was in the hospital, that they should come at once. I watched my wife get hysterical; I watched our neighbor. They ran out to the car, got in the car—I had to run to keep up with them. But I jumped into the back seat of the car. I kept trying to get my wife's attention, but every time I tried to touch her, my hand would go right through. I kept trying to tell her I wasn't in the hospital; I was right here in the back seat. As usual, she paid no attention to me.

"As they walked into the hospital, I suddenly felt a pull, and I was back in my body, in pain from the burn and the shock.

"Now that is not what's bothering me. I checked this out with my wife and my neighbor. I know that it happened exactly the way I saw it. But since then, about once a month, I find myself standing, while I'm still asleep, looking down at my body.

"What I want to know is how to stay in there! I'm not ready to go yet!"

In a reading on June 8, 1937, at Virginia Beach, for a lawyer, forty-three, who asked if he actually left his body at times to go to different places, Edgar Cayce responded:

You do.
(Q) For what purpose, and how can I develop and use this power constructively?

(A) Just as has been given as to how to enter into meditation.

Each and every soul leaves the body as it rests in sleep. As to how this may be used constructively—this would be like answering how could one use one's voice for constructive purposes. It is of a same or of a similar import, you see; that is, it is a faculty, it is an experience, it is a development of the self as related to spiritual things, material things, mental things. 853-8

Out-of-body experiences are akin to the change of consciousness we move into at the transition we call death. We have a body that travels, just as Gus Elias traveled, as the Oregon woman traveled, as the Pittsburgh man traveled, a body that survives independently of the flesh. It's part of the flesh body, integrated with it, moving with it, and in it, but faster.

This is the way Edgar Cayce put it in a reading on spirit communication on March 17, 1927, at Virginia Beach:

First, let it be understood there is the pattern in the material or physical plane of every condition as exists in the cosmic or spiritual plane, for things spiritual and things material are but those same conditions raised to a different condition [vibration] of the same element—for all force is as of one force. 5756-4

You are a soul; you have a body, Edgar Cayce said.

2

Vibration

Lots of common, everyday things are not visible to the human eye. They move too fast for perception. Some examples:

During World War II, I used to sit on planes with propellers, four big propellers. The blades would interfere with my seeing anything beyond them. Suddenly they would start the engine, and the blades would move, then blur, and disappear! They were moving so fast that I could no longer see them. I could now see the terminal on the other side of the blades. The propellers disappeared, right there in front of my eyes. We see examples of this all the time—fan blades, picket fences when we drive by fast. And we forget that our conscious perception is so limited.

Now steam is another one. You boil water, but it doesn't go anywhere; it drifts into the air. It changes form. But it's still there, as you know. We can run it through a steam engine and do work. Or we can blow a whistle. Or we can recondense it on the window, where we can't get to it as easy. When water boils away, we lose sight of it, but it's still there.

Television is another example—signals that can be turned into voices and pictures. Most of us watch television. But we can't see or hear those signals without a TV set, which is specially tuned to pick them up.

The same with radio signals—voice and music. We don't perceive these either without a radio, which can pick them up because it's tuned to receive them.

So there are patterns of matter and energy around us which we cannot perceive with our five senses—whirling propellers, liquid turned into vapor, TV and radio waves—real matter and energy, but moving or vibrating too fast for normal awareness. They are sometimes perceived unconsciously. The problem is that our perceptions usually remain unconscious, and we deny their reality because we don't perceive them. This is exactly the way with what Edgar Cayce called our finer body— or the "real body," as the readings stated.

For many years, I watched Edgar Cayce deliberately put aside physical consciousness to aid people who sought his help. He appeared to sleep; but in and from this state of sleep, his mind seemed to move in levels of consciousness far beyond the range of physical awareness. He described this sleep world. He talked with its inhabitants. He related many of his experiences.

From what we lived through with him during those years, he seemed to be a traveler in inner space. Every time he gave a reading, he seemed to depart from his body. The part of him that survives, like the part of you and me, like the part of us all that survives, was out of the body. And the readings indicated that this finer body lay just parallel to his flesh body, like a space platform, from which he could take off to seek the attunement he needed.

This is illustrated by a variety of offhand remarks he made at the start of or within certain physical readings. These remarks suggest that Edgar Cayce was actually viewing his patient and the surroundings at the exact time of the reading. Here are some examples:

4687-1: Yes, we have the body here. We have to let the body get still a minute.

3063-3: Yes, we have the body here, [3063] . . . The body is just leaving, going down in the elevator now.

168-1: (Q) . . . is this body in bed? (A) No, she is sitting in a large chair, talking to a man.

1713-1: Yes, we have the body here. We have had this before. She hasn't dressed yet, you see.

3433-1: She was in here and taken out! [reading for a patient in a sanitarium]

1683-2: Out for the walk and coming in now.

531-2: Yes, we have the body here, [531]—11:47— he has just laid aside his paper he was reading.

3853-1: (Q) What is the body doing right now . . . ? (A) Sitting in edge of window here. Quarter of twelve o'clock.

1311-1: Yes. (That's where he was yesterday [418 Cedar St.]; he's at 19 now.)

5339-1: Yes, we have the body here: Kind of busy! [He was clerking in a supermarket.]

5078-1: [Child's reading] Yes, we find the mother praying.

2969-1: Yes—(right pretty rooster!)—we have the body here, [2969].

599-10: Yes—they have had an accident right in front of the house.

2185-4: On the edge of the hill!

3079-1: Yes, little stream here . . .

5196-1: Yes, not bad-looking pajamas!

1951-1: Yes—fresh paint!

5499-1: (Too much medicine about—it smells!)

We have indexed over seven hundred statements of this type. Many were confirmed by return mail. Many more are listed in my book, *Venture Inward.* When these remarks were made, the subject of the reading was never present. At least two, often as many as five, witnesses were always present.

Some of these folks must have been shocked that Edgar Cayce, though often hundreds of miles away, was able to describe their locale or had known what they'd been doing at the exact moment of the reading.

Over the years I became acutely aware that Edgar Cayce could see and hear things that the rest of us could not.

Furthermore, Dad's mind seemed not only able to transcend space, but often also time. Mostly this happened while he was in an altered state, and then they were transcribed by Gladys Davis, his secretary, typed up and recorded. Here's one from my memory:

I was taking a bunch of Boy Scouts on an automobile trip out west, planning to camp at various national parks along the way. Before we left, I had a reading from Dad about these boys. Dad said that one of them was going to get sick in Nevada over alkali in the water, and he named the boy. He gave a prescription and said to give this boy three teaspoons of this stuff when he got sick, and he would be all right. So I had it made up before I left and carried it with me, but—you know how it is when you're in charge of boys—I forgot about it.

We had crossed the border into Nevada, camped there, got the tents set up, fixed supper, got everything shipshape, and went to sleep.

In the middle of the night another boy came and woke me and said, "Johnny is sick, just as sick as he can be. You've got to do something for him." I suddenly realized that this was the boy Dad had mentioned. So I got out my little bottle of medicine, prescribed by Dad before we left on the trip, and gave him three teaspoons of it. In a very short time, the tension went out of his face, and he completely relaxed. He went right back to sleep and slept through the rest of the night. He was perfectly all right.

Nobody else got sick, and we all drank the alkali water.

Just an amazing feat of precognition, of somebody due to get sick in Nevada over alkali in the water. And Edgar Cayce seeing it all beforehand.

But how could Dad do that? How could anyone have known about this boy's sensitivity to alkali water, known we would go there, drink it, and have known this boy would get sick, known it surely enough to prescribe an antidote beforehand? What was going on here?

Here's an instance of Edgar Cayce's precognition while awake:

(When Dad's biographer, Tom Sugrue, was writing *There Is a River,* he decided to omit this kind of story because, as he put it, people would have a hard enough time believing what Edgar Cayce did while he was asleep. Stories about what he did while awake, Sugrue contended, would make his book unbelievable.)

One day Dad and I headed into the coffee shop at the Willard Hotel in Washington, D.C., to have breakfast. A lady was standing by the door, pulling on some white gloves. We marched past her into the coffee shop, but

Dad turned, strode back, paused in front of her, then said, "Madam, if I were you, I wouldn't get into an automobile for the next twenty-four hours."

Her mouth dropped open, and she stopped pulling on her gloves. But Dad just turned and walked back into the coffee shop.

Now I couldn't get him to tell me what he saw. He just refused to talk about it. We finished breakfast and went along.

The next morning we went to the same place, and while we were sitting there, eating breakfast, this woman came through the door, hysterical, crying, wild-eyed. I knew instantly she was looking for Dad. She came rushing across to the table. I got up and tried to stop her, but she brushed past me as if I weren't there and grabbed ahold of him. He didn't even have a chance to get up.

She cried, "I want to thank you, oh, I want to thank you!"

She was incoherent, crying and sobbing. But eventually she got her story out. Within an hour after we had seen her the day before, she had been asked by her sister to go on a ride down Skyline Drive. On the strength of Dad's warning, she refused. A crumpled telegram telling of the accident was in her hand. The car had been demolished. Her sister hadn't been hurt too bad, but the woman who'd gone in her place had broken her hip.

I was astounded.

But how was this possible? Edgar Cayce must have been just seeing ahead, somehow, his mind reaching beyond the bounds, not only of space, but also of time. How could he possibly do that?

Well, I'm not sure I can tell you, but here's an explanation I first heard from my brother which suggests a possibility.

We live in a three-dimensional world. If we take a

point and move it in a direction not contained within itself, we get a line—one dimension. It can be infinitely long, but it has no width. If we move that line at right angles to itself, we get a plane—two dimensions. It has no thickness, but can be infinitely long and wide. If we move that plane at right angles to itself, we get a cube—three dimensions—the kind of world we live in.

If we could move that cube in a direction not contained within itself . . . but we cannot. We can't conceive of that. But suppose we could move it in time. Suppose it exists yesterday and today and tomorrow—past, present, and future—all at once, all in the present—but we're only conscious of the three dimensions and what seems the linear flow of time. Edgar Cayce somehow seemed to be able to move into this other dimension—a fourth dimension.

To illustrate: Suppose we have a plane—a two-dimensional plane. It has no thickness, but can be infinitely long and wide. And we have a two-dimensional bug crawling in this two-dimensional plane. It has free will and it has a memory. It remembers where it was and it knows where it is, but it can't see very far ahead. It can know very little about the future. But if our minds could somehow move into what to the bug would be a third dimension, we could sit there, look down on this plane, be able to see where the bug had been, where it is, and where it was likely to go. We could see everything that had happened to it, was happening, and could possibly happen to it in the future. And we could see this all at once.

Now this bug could never understand how we could see its past, present, and future, all at once, because it has no conception of this third dimension. But we could look at it and say, "If you continue on the way you're going, at three o'clock tomorrow you'll be right over there."

And we'd be right! But since the bug has a free will, it could decide to go somewhere else. But we could also see everything that could happen to it, what would be most probable, but we couldn't be sure what it was going to do.

If the past, present, and future all exist at once in a sort of eternal fourth-dimensional present, but the future exists as a probability, then Edgar Cayce could see what was likely to happen, but couldn't be absolutely sure, because it depends on what people do.

In a reading on April 28, 1932, at Virginia Beach, Edgar Cayce said:

> Best definition that ever may be given of fourth-dimension is an idea! Where will it project? Anywhere! Where does it arise from? Who knows! Where will it end? Who can tell! It is all inclusive! It has both length, breadth, height and depth—is without beginning and is without ending! Dependent upon that which it may feed for its sustenance, or it may pass into that much as a thought or an idea. 364-10

That timeless-spaceless dimension accessible to Edgar Cayce is accessible to all of us during sleep and meditation, he insisted. It is merely separated from our consciousness by a veil of forgetfulness. We have forgotten who we really are.

3

The Finer Body

But you don't have to be Edgar Cayce to experience this spaceless, timeless world. You and I, we, all of us, experience it every night during sleep. We're very busy in our sleep, Edgar Cayce says. We do a lot of running around in our sleep; we get out of the body, go places, do things. But we're not aware. We forget. We wipe out our memory of it because it would disturb consciousness too much, and maybe other people's consciousness, too. But if you want to and if you will apply some procedures Edgar Cayce gave us, and which I've practiced most of my life and found helpful and effective, you can learn to remember. It's a skill. It can be learned by almost anyone. The key is desire.

In fact, if you will pursue two courses that I strongly recommend—a study of your dreams and the daily practice of meditation—I will guarantee that you can discover your own finer body. You will catch yourself going and coming. When you experience this, you'll never be the same again. You'll know there are pieces and parts of you that survive; that can move away from the flesh body, and function independently of it.

If you begin to meditate, you will feel it and sense the movement of this finer body, for it is what moves when you meditate—back and forth, around, circular; the expansion, the extension. You will feel this when you learn to meditate. Many of you may have already had such experiences. This finer body is the body we're talking about. This is the body that survives. This is the body with which you have perception in those odd moments, during sleep sometimes and following the change we call "death."

Sleep, Cayce said, is a shadow of that intermission in earth's experience of that state called death. Death is like sleep, in a sense, which, if you stop to think about it, is not such a wild statement. Jesus says the same thing:

> And he cometh to the house of the ruler of the synagogue, and seeth the tumult, and them that wept and wailed greatly.
> And when he was come in, he saith unto them, Why make ye this ado, and weep? the damsel is not dead, but sleepeth.   (Mark 5:38-39 KJV)

Then Jesus took her by the hand, told her to arise, and she got up and walked.

Again, later:

> . . . Our friend Lazarus sleepeth; but I go, that I may awake him out of sleep.

Then said his disciples, Lord, if he sleep, he shall do well.

Howbeit Jesus spake of his death: but they thought that he had spoken of taking of rest in sleep.

Then said Jesus unto them plainly, Lazarus is dead.   (John 11:11-14 KJV)

This finer body is what Jesus used to resurrect His flesh body. Scripture recounts many instances of people seeing Him after the resurrection—Mary Magdalene, when she thought He was the gardener, and He said, "Touch me not; for I am not yet ascended to my Father..." (John 20:17); then Cleopas and Simon on the road to Emmaus, who tarried with Him awhile before they realized who He was (Luke 24:18); then the disciples and others in the upper room (John 20:19; Luke 24:33); Thomas, who wouldn't believe until he examined His wounds (John 20:26); later the disciples at the Sea of Tiberias when Jesus directed them to the fish and asked Peter three times, "Lovest thou me?" Peter answering, "Yea, Lord, thou knowest that I love thee," and Jesus saying, "Feed my sheep . . . feed my lambs . . . follow me" (John 21:15-17). Finally, those who watched His ascension from Mt. Olivet (Acts 1:9). There were probably others.

Personally, I have no doubt about these reports, because I have seen Jesus myself, more than once.

The first experience was when I was a teenager. It turned my life around.

I saw Him again in the late 1940s, not long after Dad died and I had returned from World War II. I was on a speaking tour for the A.R.E., which had only a few hundred members then. I was in Dallas at the home of Rudolph Johnson—our attorney—and set to address a gathering of about forty. But I had become ill and had to go to bed. I was delirious and burning up with fever. We called a doctor; he gave me a penicillin shot. Johnson wanted to call off the meeting, but the people were already there. I decided to go ahead with it.

Somehow I dragged myself out of bed. Somehow I managed to start talking. I could feel the penicillin working. I haven't the least idea what I said, but suddenly a figure appeared on my left. I thought first it was my father. But as I stared, I saw it was Jesus. He grinned, laughed at me really, and said, "It is I. You needn't be afraid." He reached out and touched me on the shoulder. That touch was like a shock, a lightning bolt. Instantly, I was drenched in sweat. I stopped talking, wasn't saying a thing, just standing there, gawking. And my fever broke. The people in the room didn't know what was happening, but some later said they felt something electric. Then He smiled at me and said, "Now, get to work." From that point on, I couldn't do anything that didn't work. Anything! I'd call people up and ask them to do something, and they'd do it. I couldn't say anything, write anything that didn't work. Even my mistakes worked! From that point on, I never thought I was working for the A.R.E.—I was working for Jesus.

4

The Light

When Edgar Cayce gave a reading, it was necessary for him to see an inner light. He would put his hands over his forehead and, when he saw this light, move them to his solar plexus, cross them, and take two or three deep diaphragm breaths, from the abdomen. His eyelids would flutter, and you had to talk to him right then, while those eyelids were fluttering. If you did not do this, he'd just go to sleep, and you'd miss him. He'd just go to sleep for an hour or two. He seemed to take advantage of those times when you missed him!

Afterward, he'd wake up hungry, wanting a cracker and a glass of milk, feeling fine, thinking he'd given a reading. Because, you see, in all those forty-three years

of giving readings, he never heard one word he said in
that altered state.

Once we asked Edgar Cayce in his altered state why he
didn't remember; he said:

> ... if the body ... were to be wholly conscious of
> that through which it passes in its *soul's* activity ...
> the strain would be so great upon that which holds
> the mental ... in order ... as to become demented
> in its relationship. And he is thought crazy enough
> anyway! 5756-14

Now the light that Dad needed was a flash of white
light. It was an indication to him that his soul was able to
attune itself to those finer realms.

In a reading on November 17, 1943, at Virginia Beach,
for a woman, fifty, this reference was made:

> Thus the son of man came into the earth, made
> in the form, the likeness of man; with body, mind,
> soul. Yet the soul was the Son, the soul was the
> Light. 3357-2

A reading for a minister and musician, twenty-three,
on August 31, 1943, at Virginia Beach, stated:

> Then, it is necessary for the reliance upon Him,
> who is the truth and the light, who from the begin-
> ning was that expressed in, "And God said, let there
> be light: and there was light." 3188-1

After seeing this flash of white light, after giving the
reading, sometimes, actually seventeen times in all
those thousands of readings, he'd remember a dream
when he returned to consciousness, always about the

same. Here's his version of it:

> I see myself as a tiny dot out of my physical body, which lies inert before me. I find myself oppressed by darkness, and there is a feeling of terrific loneliness. Suddenly, I am conscious of a white beam of light. As this tiny dot, I move upward, following the light, knowing that I must follow it or be lost.
>
> As I move along this path of light, I gradually become conscious of various levels upon which there is movement. Upon the first levels there are vague, horrible shapes—grotesque forms such as one sees in nightmares. As I pass on, there begin to appear on either side misshapen forms of human beings, with some part of the body magnified.
>
> Again there is a change, and I become conscious of gray-hooded forms moving downward. Gradually these become lighter in color. Then the direction changes, and these forms move upward—and the color of the robes grows rapidly lighter.
>
> Next, there begin to appear on each side vague outlines of houses, walls, trees, etc., but everything is motionless. As I pass on, there is more light and movement in what appear to be normal cities and towns. With the growth of movement, I become conscious of sounds—at first indistinct rumblings, then music, laughter, and the singing of birds. There is more and more light; the colors become very beautiful; and there is a blending of sound and color.
>
> Quite suddenly, I come upon a hall of records. It is a hall without walls, without a ceiling; but I am conscious of seeing an old man who hands me a large book—a record of the individual for whom I seek information.

According to this dream, while following a beam of white light, Edgar Cayce saw entities occupying various planes with respect to their development. A mental attunement could be set up with any of those within the range of what Edgar Cayce called "the sphere of communication."

We find another reference to the differences in states of consciousness at death in a reading given on June 17, 1933, for about thirty attending the second A.R.E. Congress at Virginia Beach.

(Q) Describe some of the planes into which entities pass on experiencing the change called death.

(A) Passing from the material consciousness to a spiritual or cosmic, or outer consciousness, oft does an entity or being not become conscious of that about it; much in the same manner as an entity born into the material plane only becomes conscious gradually of that designated as time and space for the material or third dimensional plane. In the passage the entity becomes conscious, or the recognition of being in a fourth or higher dimensional plane takes place, much in the same way as the consciousness is gained in the material.

For, as we have given, that we see manifested in the material plane is but a shadow of that in the spiritual plane.

In materiality we find some advance faster, some grow stronger, some become weaklings. Until there is redemption through the acceptance of the law (or love of God, as manifested through the Channel or the Way), there can be little or no development in a material or spiritual plane. But all must pass under the rod, even as He—who entered into materiality. 5749-3

One morning, in our house on Fourteenth Street, Virginia Beach, when Dad came down to breakfast—you never knew what was coming out of this man, even from his regular sleep—he said that he'd heard this tapping on the second-floor window as he was climbing into bed. It was a young woman who had died in Selma, Alabama. "Bunchie," he called her. She had once worked for him in the photo studio there.

Bunchie had contracted a throat infection and been operated on by a doctor in Selma. But she had died. Someone wrote us about it, and we saw this in the paper. Dad wrote to the family, and so forth; we knew the family well.

Now, Bunchie was a very proper young lady. She wouldn't enter my parents' bedroom, but stayed outside and tapped on the window. Dad said he heard Bunchie saying, "Won't you please come down and let me in?"

So Dad went down, opened the door, and she exclaimed, "I am so glad to see you! I've been looking everywhere for you! I've had such a terrible time finding you! I'm dead, I know I'm dead! And I don't know what to do."

He said, "Come in." And she went in, and sat down, and he talked to her. Dad said he could see through her.

Meanwhile, Mother heard voices and became curious. She wondered who Dad was talking to in the middle of the night. She came to the head of the stairs. Nobody was there but Dad, talking to this girl in his head. Yet Mother heard two voices.

Now as Dad talked to this girl, she told him a fantastic story:

She said she had died under the operation, and didn't immediately get better after she died. She still suffered for a time, she said. But it wasn't very long before the doctor died, came "over," completed the operation successfully, and broke it to her gently that she was dead. She got better then and went home to her mother's and father's house, who were also dead; but they were gone a lot. They kept leaving, and she wasn't able to go with them. Worse, she couldn't seem to communicate with them or get them to listen to her. She felt abandoned, alone.

There were valid reasons for her plight, it seems. She had unintentionally backed herself into a corner with preconceived notions about death while she was alive, notions she didn't discuss with her parents. It seems that, if we can communicate over here, we can communicate over there. It's a matter of interest and concern. If we love here, then love continues over there.

Not knowing what to do, but thinking Edgar Cayce might help, Bunchie came looking for him at his old photo studio in Selma. She hung around until she overheard someone say that Edgar Cayce had gone to Virginia Beach. So she came to Virginia Beach and finally found him.

During their talk downstairs, Dad said, "Have you seen the light? Do you remember the light?"

She said, "I used to see a light."

So he talked to her about this, explained to her exactly what she had to do, how she could see and follow the light again. He prayed with her and told her he'd ask the group to pray for her. He taught her how to release herself from her earthbound condition and move forward. She went away after that, content, he decided, because he never heard from her again.

Interesting that Dad sensed her presence when he was getting ready for bed. Likewise, the California woman who traveled out-of-body to see her grandchild in Oregon was taking a nap. Both Bunchie and the California woman used their finer bodies to go someplace, but one was dead, the other alive.

The light Dad saw when he gave readings is the same light you will see in meditation, a light which, when we follow it, lets us move through these levels and states of consciousness. Meditation, then, becomes a way of setting us upon what *The Secret of the Golden Flower* terms the Tao, or Way, freeing us from the endless cycle of incarnations. In meditation we come to know this light, sense it, become it. It is a light available to all of us.

5

The Silver Cord

The readings tell us that, while giving readings, Edgar Cayce remained connected to his flesh body by a "silver cord." We disturbed this connection on some occasions by passing things across his abdomen—not often, because when we did this, we couldn't wake him up. When somebody moved something across his abdomen, he quit talking, right in the midst of a reading. This occurred once when I was conducting a reading, and went on for an hour. First I tried to get him to continue, then to wake him up. During this time he showed no sign, even, of life. I was getting deeply concerned. And people in the room were getting frantic. Then, he came out of it, swiftly, following a suggestion, and was suddenly standing straight up, and visibly upset.

We asked questions after that, took readings on it.

In a reading given on September 7, 1933, at Virginia Beach, we asked him what had happened:

> To the *body*, little. To the *mental* forces, or the spiritual activity of the entity as a whole, a very hard *knock;* as there was the *desire* to enter in, and the entity stumbled—as it were—against a closed door. 254-67

In another reading that afternoon, Cayce was asked:

> (Q) What caused the extraordinary physical reaction with Edgar Cayce at the close of the reading [254-67] this morning, at the beginning of the suggestion [that he awaken]?
>
> (A) As was seen, through the seeking of irrelevant questions there was antagonism manifested. This made for a contraction of those channels through which the activity of the psychic forces operates in the material body; as we have outlined, along the pineal, the lyden and the cord—or silver cord. The natural reactions are for sudden contraction when changing suddenly from the mental-spiritual to material.
>
> For, as evidenced by that which has been given, there is the touching—with the mental beings of those present in the room or at such manifestations—of the most delicate mechanism that may be well imagined.
>
> As has been crudely given, a hen may lay an egg but the shell once cracked or broken *cannot* be made to produce that it contains.
>
> When the thought, the activity that is being made

manifest, is broken, that which is creative or constructive—once touched by thought or suggestion—is hindered, wavered, as to that it may bring
to a manifested form.

Hence the experiences that are sometimes held,
or that may be held, by those that may witness or
experience the transmission of that which is received or gained through this particular channel,
may—by the mere disturbing of the body that rests
above the natural body by other than the elements
that have not taken bodily form—break the associations, the connections, with that source from
which the records are being taken. 254-68

Note "the body that rests above the natural body," by
which Cayce meant this finer body that permeates us all.

Once, during a reading, Dad told us that, at the end of
the reading, if we watched closely, we could see his soul
returning to his flesh body. Well, I watched, but I couldn't
see it. Maybe others did; I didn't.

People who came for readings over the years were often curious about what Dad did, what was going on
when Dad put his hands over his forehead, moved them
to his solar plexus, crossed them, took two or three deep
breaths, then, eyelids fluttering, went to sleep. In a reading on February 3, 1934, at the Zentgraf home on Staten
Island, Mrs. Eileen Garrett, medium for Uvani, her spirit
guide, asked:

(Q) Would you explain why Edgar Cayce uses this
method of hypnosis for going into trance?

(A) That as has oft been given, from the physical
development, or physical-mental development of
the body, it has become necessary that there be the
entire removal of the physical forces and physical

attributes from the mental and spiritual and soul forces of the entity, to seek that through that built in the *soul*-body of the entity it may contact that which may be constructive in the experiences of those to whom such sources or such supplies of information may be brought.

(Q) How did it arise? Was it accident, or some entity or group suggest this plan?

(A) Soul development, rather. And the ability to, through those experiences in the earth in the varied activities, lay aside the consciousness that the soul and the spirit and the truth might find its way through to the seeker.

(Q) Do you suggest that trance is a useful method for help?

(A) Trance to the individual is as the necessary stimuli for each soul in its own development. There be those who may through their intuitive activity, that has subjugated the influences in the material, allow the mental soul to manifest. There be those who through looking into the past, or into the aura, or into all or any of those things that are as witnesses about every soul that walks through this vale. For, those that may lay aside the veil, in whatever form or manner, may make for the approach of aiding those in seeking to know that necessary in their development in the present experience. 507-1

6

Sleep

So in sleep and after death, activities and experiences go on. Some of our most vivid and exciting experiences take place in sleep. Many of us have had dreams more vivid than anything that's happened to us in this life. Certainly comparable to anything in this life.

We asked Dad to enlighten us about what happens when we sleep or, as he put it, "lay aside the veil," (507-1) in a reading on July 14, 1932, in Virginia Beach.

> First, we would say, sleep is a shadow of, that intermission in earth's experiences of, that state called death . . . 5754-1

He continued this discourse in another reading the next day:

> Sleep—that period when the soul takes stock of that it has acted upon during one rest period to another, making or drawing—as it were—the comparisons that make for Life itself in its *essence,* as for harmony, peace, joy, love, long-suffering, patience, brotherly love, kindness—these are the fruits of the Spirit. 5754-2

Again, that afternoon, he continued:

> Now, as we have that condition that exists with the body and this functioning, or this sense, or this ability of sleep and sense, or a sixth sense, just what, how, may this knowledge be used to advantage for an individual's development towards that it would attain?
> As to how it may be used, then, depends upon what is the ideal of that individual; for, as has been so well pointed out in Holy Writ, if the ideal of the individual is lost, then the abilities for that faculty or that sense of an individual to contact the spiritual forces are gradually lost, or barriers are builded that prevent this from being a sensing of the nearness of an individual to a spiritual development.
> As to those who are nearer the spiritual realm, their visions, dreams, and the like, are more often— and are more often retained by the individual; for, as is seen as a first law, it is self-preservation. 5754-3

Some asked Cayce for insight into their own sleep experiences.

Mrs. Morton Blumenthal, twenty-one, sought interpretation of a dream in which she said to Edwin, her brother-in-law, "Now, you see, death is not the grave as many people think—it is another phenomenized form of life." In a reading at Virginia Beach on November 11, 1925, Edgar Cayce commented:

And the entity then sees, through the subconscious forces, that death is as but the beginning of another form of phenomenized force in the earth's plane, and may not be understood by the third dimension mind from third dimension analysis, but must be seen from that fourth-dimension force as may be experienced by an entity gaining the access to same, by development in the physical plane through the mental processes of an entity. The mind is being correlated with subconscious and spiritual forces that magnify same to the conscious force of an entity in such a manner as said entity gains the insight and concept of such phenomenized conditions, see? 136-18

Note the phrase, "may be experienced."

In a reading on January 4, 1926, at Virginia Beach, Mrs. Edwin Blumenthal, twenty-three, sought counsel on a dream:

(Q) "Next, Edwin, my mother and myself were sitting in a room, I in my blue wrapper. I knew I was dead, yet there I was seated just as I do today, dressed and looking the same as in physical life and I was wondering if anyone knew that I was there, if they knew what I knew—that I had been killed. I could see them and myself, but could they see me?—know I was sitting there and also know that I myself, even though dead, knew of my own presence—of my own consciousness? I was sitting next to Edwin caressing him—loving him just the same as before. Just then my Aunt Lily [. . .] came into the room and spoke to my mother and Edwin. Now I realized that this would be my proof as to whether they knew of my presence or not. Aunt Lily [. . .] looked directly at the chair upon which I was seated, but she did not see me—to her I was not there!"

(A) This again shows that same force as given in that concept of the preparation necessary in the physical that each may understand that connection which lies between the physical and the spiritual, that such a condition as viewed and experienced by the entity in this vision may be in that way and manner as to be able to bridge this chasm. That is, that the consciousness of this entity is gaining in this vision a concept of what is called physical death, and that the consciousness, with all its earthly ties, so long as it (that consciousness) remains in the earth's plane, it (that consciousness) is cognizant of that condition taking place in the physical, see? and is then the spiritual action. Then the lesson is as given. The entity should gain from this that concept of the great truths which are gained from the subconscious forces which are being manifest in the physical world, that the full consciousness of self's projection from the subconscious, or death plane, may even be understood, comprehended, in the physical. 140-10

7

God's Other Door

So what is death? What does Edgar Cayce say about it?

Remember the premise we've already established: You are a soul; you have a body.

This flesh body, then, is not our real body. Our real body is this finer body that vibrates too fast for normal perception. To see it we need to speed up our own vibration, which we do by praying, meditating, trying to manifest the fruits of the spirit, or remembering our dreams. Or we can see it if we encounter someone like Jesus, who can make Himself visible, tangible, by slowing the vibrations of His finer body to match ours.

As we grasp this concept, these quotes from the

readings begin to make sense.

In a reading at the David Kahn home in Scarsdale, New York, on November 13, 1937, a woman, fifty-seven, writer, radio broadcaster, Protestant, was told:

> Death—as commonly spoken of—is only passing through God's other door. 1472-2

In a reading on August 11, 1935, at Norfolk, Virginia, while writing the lesson, "Destiny of the Body," Search for God Study Group #1 asked:

> (Q) At the change called death is the entity free of a physical or material body?
> (A) Free of the material body but not free of matter; only changed in the form as to matter; and is just as acute to the realms of consciousness as in the physical or material or carnal body, or more so. 262-86

In other words, he's saying that this finer body is good at sensation, good at perception. Extended perception, if you will. Not blanked out at all. It is actually still a body, still matter, of atomic structure. But it's moving faster than our flesh bodies, so we cannot ordinarily see it.

In a reading for a restaurant manager, thirty-three, Hebrew, on August 18, 1937, at Virginia Beach, Edgar Cayce said:

> For, as has been given, it is not all of life to live, nor yet all of death to die. For life and death are one, and only those who will consider the experience as one may come to understand or comprehend what peace indeed means. 1977-1

Only when you begin to try to look at life and death as
a continuity, a stream of experience, of consciousness,
only then can you begin to deal with peace, in its essence. For, when you fear death, life can be a very chal-
lenging experience.

Now, this will be clarified, but let me restate it. What
Edgar Cayce is saying is that you're going to deal exactly,
when you die, with what you create, in your mind, the
world of thought-forms, that you build, the attachment,
the thought, the kind of activity you're going to get involved in, the moment you pass.

In a reading for a woman, thirty-one, Christian, on
August 16, 1935, at Virginia Beach, Edgar Cayce said:

> . . . a death in the flesh is a birth into the realm of
> another experience, to those who have lived in such
> a manner as not to be bound by earthly ties. This
> does not mean that it does not have its own experi-
> ence about the earth, but that it has lived such a
> *fullness* of life that it must be about its business.
> 989-2

For those who have lived right, it's a birth into another
experience, another dimension. And just as we die here,
we're born there. And we die there, we're born here. It is a
door; another of God's doors.

In a reading on January 3, 1925, at Dayton, Ohio,
Morton Blumenthal asked:

> (Q) What happens to the conscious mind forces
> and physical forces at death?
> (A) The conscious mind forces either are in the
> soul's development, and in the superconsciousness,
> or left with that portion of material forces which
> goes to the reclaiming, or remoulding, of physical

bodies, for indwelling of spiritual entities. 900-17

Morton Blumenthal, on January 15, 1925, at the Cambridge Hotel in New York City, asked:

> (Q) Explain the plane of spirit and soul forces, and what relation this plane has to earth. You will start with death, as we know it.
> (A) In that moment—as in birth we have the beginning of an earthly sojourn, little or long, as time may be—as the birth into the spiritual plane begins with the death in earth plane; merely the separation of the spiritual and soul forces from the earthly connections. 900-19

In a previously quoted reading, on June 17, 1933, for thirty attending the second A.R.E. Congress at Virginia Beach, Edgar Cayce said:

> . . . *death* . . . is only a transition—or through God's other door—into that realm where the entity has builded, in its manifestations as related to the knowledge and activity respecting the law of the universal influence . . .
> Death in the material plane is passing through the outer door into a consciousness in the material activities that partakes of what the entity, or soul, has done with its spiritual truth in its manifestations in other sphere. 5749-3

At a reading in Rye, New York, on November 29, 1941, Edgar Cayce told an actress and drama teacher, fifty-two, Catholic:

> It is not all of life, then, to live, nor all of death to

die; but what the entity does *with* the opportunities as they present themselves. 2630-1

In a life reading on August 19, 1927, at Virginia Beach, a woman, thirty-eight, was told:

> ... develop toward that mark of higher calling as is set in Him—for it is not all of life to live, nor all of death to die; for one is the beginning of the other, and in the midst of life one is in the midst of death—in death one begins in that birth into which the earthly application of the inmost intents and desires as applied in respect to will's forces, that given by the Creative Energy, that one might make self equal with that Energy. 2842-2

Morton Blumenthal, in a life reading given on March 6, 1929, at Virginia Beach, was told:

> For life, in its continuity, is that experience of the soul or entity—including its soul, its spirit, its superconscious, its subconscious, its physical consciousness, or its *material* consciousness, in that as its *development* goes through the various experiences takes on more and more that ability of knowing itself to be itself, yet a portion of the great whole, or the one Creative Energy that is in and through all. 900-426

In a reading on June 20, 1944, at Virginia Beach, a stockbroker, forty-six, was told:

> For what profiteth a man who does gain the whole world and loseth his own soul? Or what would ye gain in exchange for the awareness of thy

soul, that ye may know life is indeed eternal; and it
isn't then all of life to live, nor all of death to die.
3436-2

In a reading on August 9, 1936, at Virginia Beach, a
business woman, advertising agent, and Christian, fifty-
two, asked:

(Q) Must I go on living?
(A) Life is eternal. It is in Him, and merely to
change through God's other door has only changed
the outlook. But as we prepare the self for the vistas
of the various consciousness[es] upon the stages of
development, we become a part of that—if our
pathway is being led aright. 1246-2

In a reading on December 2, 1932, at Virginia Beach, a
housewife, twenty-four, Hebrew, asked:

(Q) How can I desire to live more than to die, especially during two weeks or more of every month
. . . When I desire death more than life, how can I
use my will?
(A) When desire for death and the desire for life is
presented, what is it that makes the life go on? The
will! The spiritual life, the essence of God itself!
Would the body be so weak as to crucify that it worships, rather than that which is only tagged on—in
desires? . . .
In lightening the burden of another thine own is
lightened twofold. In lightening the burdens of another the whole of will's power is strengthened
manyfold. 911-7

There was much more to this reading and other readings, physical, mental, and spiritual, for this woman, but, tragically, she took her own life six years later at age thirty, David Kahn indicated in a note, June 1938.

For Search for God Group #1, writing the lesson, "Destiny," July 21, 1935, in Norfolk, Virginia, Edgar Cayce said:

> How is the way shown by the Master? What is the promise in Him? The last to be overcome is death. Death of what?
>
> The *soul* cannot die; for it is of God. The body may be revivified, rejuvenated. And it is to that end it may, the body, *transcend* the earth and its influence.
>
> But not those standing here may reach it yet! 262-85

On October 18, 1930, while Edgar Cayce was giving a reading, he had another unusual dream:

> I was preparing to give a reading. As I went out, I realized that I had contacted Death, as a personality, as an individual, as a being. I remarked to Death: "You are not as ordinarily pictured—with a black mask or hood, or as a skeleton, or like Father Time with a sickle. Instead, you are fair, rose-cheeked, robust—and you have a pair of shears or scissors." In fact, I had to look twice at the feet or limbs; or even at the body, to see it take shape.
>
> He replied: "Yes, Death is not what many seem to think. It is not the horrible thing which is often pictured. Just a change—just a visit. The shears or scissors are indeed the implements most representative of life and death to man. These indeed unite by dividing—and divide by uniting. The cord does not, as usually thought, extend from the center—but is

broken from the head, the forehead—that soft portion we see pulsate in the infant. Hence we see old people, unbeknowing to themselves, gain strength from youth by kissing there: and youth gains wisdom by such kisses.

Indeed the vibrations may be raised to such an extent as to rekindle or reconnect the cord, even as the Master did with the son of the widow of Nain. For He did not take him by the hand (which was bound to the body as was the custom of the day), but rather stroked him on the head—and the body took life of Life itself! So, you see, the silver cord may be broken—but vibration ... "

Here the dream ended.

Remember that Jesus was asked about life after death by the man He was being crucified with. And He said, "This day you'll be with me in paradise." (Luke 23:43) In a reading on January 12, 1936, in Norfolk, Virginia, for Search for God Study Group #1, during the lesson, "Glory," Edgar Cayce described what He meant by paradise:

The inter-between; the awareness of being in that state of transition between the material and the spiritual phases of consciousness of the Soul. The awareness that there is the companionship of entities or souls, or separate forces in those stages of the development. 262-92

It seems fallacious to reduce death to a common denominator. It is very individual, very personal. Awareness in the transition period differs with each entity. Other differences and similarities may be noted.

In a previously quoted reading that was given at the David Kahn home in Scarsdale, New York, on November

13, 1937, a woman, fifty-seven, writer, radio broadcaster,
Protestant, asked:

(Q) Does death instantly end all feeling in the
physical body? If not, how long can it feel?

(A) This would be such a problem; dependent
upon the character of which unconsciousness is
produced to the physical reaction—or the manner
in which the consciousness has been trained [to
think about death].

Death—as commonly spoken of—is only passing
through God's other door. That there is continued
consciousness is evidenced, ever, by . . . the abilities
of entities to project or to make those impressions
upon the consciousness of sensitives or the like.

As to how long [death may take]—many an individual has remained in that called death for what
ye call *years* without realizing it was dead!

The feelings, the desires for what ye call appetites
are changed, or not aware at all. The ability to communicate is that which usually disturbs or worries
others.

Then, as to say how long—that depends upon the
entity.

For as has been given, the psychic forces of an
entity are *constantly* active—whether the soul-entity is aware of same or not. Hence as has been the
experience of many, these become as individual as
individualities or personalities are themselves.

(Q) If cremated, would the body feel it?

(A) What body?

The physical body is not the consciousness. The
consciousness of the physical body is a separate
thing. There is the mental body, the physical body,
the spiritual body.

As has so oft been given, what is the builder? *Mind!* Can you burn or cremate a mind? Can you destroy the physical body? Yes, easily. To be absent (what is absent?) from the body is to be present with the Lord, or the universal consciousness, or the ideal. Absent from what? What absent? Physical consciousness, yes.

As to how long it requires to lose physical consciousness depends upon how great are the *appetites* and desires of a physical body! 1472-2

8

Ghosts

Often, especially in later years, when Dad gave talks to church or A.R.E. groups, he'd welcome "those standing in the back"—the dead ones, the "spirit entities" who were also part of the audience. Some of the live ones never knew whether or not to take him seriously. But as time passed, and I heard him do this again and again, I came to realize he was dead serious, if you'll pardon the pun.

As I've indicated, growing up with Edgar Cayce was like living with a microscope or telescope. You know, if you look at a drop of water with your naked eye, it looks like just a drop of water; but a microscope reveals all kinds of things crawling around. Likewise, if you look at the night sky with your naked eye, you see just stars; but a telescope reveals planets, nebulae, comets—all kinds of unimaginable objects.

My grandfather, my father's father, "L. B., the Squire," lived with us in Virginia Beach. While visiting my aunt, my father's sister, in Hopkinsville, Kentucky, he died. Only Dad went to the funeral; the rest of us stayed home. About three days after Dad returned, my grandfather showed up in Virginia Beach.

Now, he was dead—we couldn't see him. But we could hear him! He had asthma; we could hear him breathing. Everybody in the house could hear him, plus the postman and other visitors. It was weird, believe me! But Dad insisted that he was just straightening out his papers and that he was going on very soon, but had left some things undone. He hadn't planned on dying and had come back. He was just straightening things up.

Now, nothing ever moved in the room, Dad said, but I didn't believe him! I kept running upstairs, looking in the room. I thought it was rats, or mice, or something. But it would make real noises. And Dad kept telling me to leave him alone, that I was going to disturb him, and that he'd go away in a little bit.

One day I collared the postman. He delivered the mail at the front door. He knew my grandfather, used to chat with him. I dragged him inside and said, "Listen, you tell me what you hear." I let him listen. And upstairs at that time you could hear my grandfather moving in his room, a shuffling, floorboards creaking.

The postman said, "What in the world? Is somebody up there?" I said, "Yeah, my grandfather." His eyes opened wide and he said, "I thought your grandfather was dead!"

"He is," I assured him.

At which, he turned about as white as a sheet, then

left—and from then on delivered the mail at the gate. He wouldn't come into the yard after that.

A short time later I was at a luncheon with my mother and Gladys Davis, my father, my brother, and we heard those noises. Everybody heard them. And I said, "I've got to go up there." Dad said, "If I were you, I wouldn't do it." But I went anyway, jumped up, and ran upstairs. I didn't get all the way. I got up to the landing—and ran into my grandfather. I went through him, in a way. It was like running into cobwebs across a path at night—if you've ever walked in the woods. It was around you. I was absolutely convinced that that was what it was. And he was cold.

Every hair on my head stood straight up, in broad daylight. I was frightened, caught by surprise on the landing where I didn't expect him.

He was leaving then, I think, because he never showed up again. I felt a little bad, as if maybe I'd pushed him away too soon; but Dad said no, that that wasn't true.

Another time, much later, I came in late from a lecture, turned on the television for the news, and the phone rang. It was a navy captain, in Churchland. And he was frightened.

He said, "I've been told that you might be able to help me. We have a ghost in our house, I think. I don't know what to do about it. And they told me you wouldn't laugh at me."

The next day, he, his wife, a six-year-old girl, and a baby in her mother's arms—all four—arrived in my office. And I heard a bizarre story.

They had rented an old house in Churchland, cheap, and that surprised them. It hadn't been occupied for some time, and the Realtor seemed anxious. Almost immediately after they moved in, they began to hear strange sounds, a thump, like a bag being dropped, and then a noise, as if something were being pulled or moved. And then the lock, the latch on the door in the master bedroom, would begin to rattle, but did not move. Now, this is wild!

They had a cat and a dog. The cat had left; the dog was cowed, and was between the wife's knees all the time. The little six-year-old girl became hysterical, and they had moved into another bedroom in the house. They were isolated, practically, and this would happen, not every night, but frequently; that thump, and the pulling, and the cracking of the lock, which was one of those that you push down on, and it lifts the latch, and makes a noise. They went out, asked around the neighborhood, and discovered the story about it.

There was a man and woman who had lived there, and the man had a tendency to drink heavily, and he beat his wife. One night, she put everything in a suitcase and left him. He was drunk, and became despondent, and tried to shoot himself; he didn't do a very good job, and crawled off the bed, and got his hand onto the lock.

That's where they found him, about four days later. He apparently had been crawling to that door, right from the beginning, and kept crawling every night. I don't know why.

After hearing this story, as might be expected, the captain and his wife had had more strange experiences. They described soft tappings on various pieces of furniture, the dragging of a heavy soft object, a clatter in the fireplace set, a thumping in the upstairs hall, and a darkening and staining of the bedroom rug.

Talking at length with them, I recommended prayer for several days in succession. I told them I'd get a prayer group to aid them during the same period, and I did. I suggested positively that they wouldn't be disturbed further, and that, if they were, I would come to their house personally and stay there myself to observe.

At the end of a week, the captain called to say they'd

heard no more noises. I urged him to redecorate, paint and clean the upper bedroom. A month later he called again to report no further difficulty.

So the transition period from life to death is not the same for everyone. It varies greatly from person to person. It depends, as we shall see, upon what you have done with your life, upon what you are thinking about, what you're building for yourself, mentally, spiritually, on a day-to-day basis.

Now, time doesn't seem to matter much. "The first ten minutes after death" could be a long time for some of us. There is no time, no space in that other dimension. Movement over there is instantaneous, as quick as thought, and time is all one. So, how long will death take? Cayce said:

> . . . many an individual has remained in that called death for what ye call *years* without realizing it was dead! 1472-2

That's a strange statement, but it gives us good reason, not just for this life, but the continuity of life, to try to follow a more lighted path, for that light shines right through this life, and into the next.

Years ago, when I was a kid in Selma, Alabama, I was party to another strange experience with the man who lived across the street. The kids said he was a miser. I delivered papers there. He was a grumpy old gentleman, worked in the cotton exchange, and was supposed to have a lot of money. He had an apartment across the street from us, downtown. Our apartment was over the studio.

One night we heard him moaning and groaning. He had stomach pains. He had big strong doors on his apartment. Someone called the fire department, but the doors were locked. They couldn't break them down. They had to climb in the window. Before they could get to him, he died. And he died screaming and hollering.

Many years later in Virginia Beach, Dad was giving a reading for someone in Selma and casually threw into the end of the reading, "Mr. So-and-So," naming that old gentleman, "has just become aware that he's dead."

Now that's what I'd call a "long" ten minutes.

These are just a few cases that have come to my attention. Thousands more have occurred in the annals of psychic research. They're reported by thousands of witnesses from all over the world. One or two just might be reliable. But if they make you uncomfortable, I can easily get rid of them for you. I can relieve you of thinking about them entirely.

You can label them hearsay, assume they're just stories, rumors handed down in these families, inadvertently doctored while being retold, certain details omitted, others made up, warped or reshaped to suit the teller's sense of mystery and drama. You can say they lack authenticity, that they're not scientific, not verifiable. You can attack the character of the so-called witnesses. Or you may want to concoct a sort of a psychic residue, something left over, maybe a thought-form, not necessarily a ghost. Maybe the result of oversensitivity or overactive imagination. Maybe these weren't ghosts at all. Just thought-forms.

Of course, it's your prerogative to think about these things any way you want. Or not to think about them, just as you choose. For me it was different. I grew up with them. And my prerogative was to take them for just what they seemed to me—ghosts.

You know, this whole business of death and dying is an interesting business; and the first ten minutes is apparently a delightful and exciting time for most of us.

My stories about my grandfather, my grandmother, Bunchie, the old miser, and the drinking and shooting, and so forth, were given for the purpose of focusing your mind on someone who got trapped in a sort of time warp, where things continue over and over. Hence, the importance of meditation, of finding that shaft of light, that path we can travel on, and move through some of these planes of existence.

9

Thoughts

In a reading given on June 16, 1933, at Virginia Beach, for the second A.R.E. Congress, Edgar Cayce said:

The mind is the builder ever, whether in the spirit or in the flesh. If one's mind is filled with those things that bespeak of the spirit, that one becomes spiritual-minded.

As we may find in a material world: Envy, strife, selfishness, greediness, avarice, are the children of *man!* Long-suffering, kindness, brotherly love, good deeds, are the children of the spirit of light.

Choose ye (as it has ever been given) whom ye will serve.

This is not beggaring the question! As individuals become abased, or possessed, are their thoughts guided by those in the borderland? Certainly! If allowed to be!

But he that looks within is higher, for the spirit knoweth the Spirit of its Maker—and the children of same are as given. And, "My Spirit beareth witness with thy spirit," saith He that giveth life! 5753-1

Let's see now—I forget the year—about 1939, I think, I decided that the Cadillac was by far the most beautiful car on the market. I wished that I could have a Cadillac. I didn't wish very strong for it, but I did wish. I don't remember what kind of car we had at the time—probably a Ford. But I thought a Cadillac would be ideal. That was the kind of car I wanted. I might have even gone around and looked at some Cadillacs—not because I had anything to buy them with, but because that was the kind of car I wanted.

Then about 1951, a dozen or so years later, somebody gave me a Cadillac, just gave it to me. Called me one day and said, "Hugh Lynn, here's a car I do not need. Wouldn't you like to have it?" And it was a 1939 Cadillac!

This business of visualization is a tricky one. We're dealing with the thought realm where every idle thought takes form. Every criticism, every negative thought registers and has effect. Not an idle word, not an idle thought that doesn't go into a bank that will someday look us straight in the face. I've restated what Edgar Cayce said, that the subconscious mind becomes the consciousness the moment we step out of this body. To figure out what that consciousness is going to be like, just look at the subconscious mind. Look squarely at it!

You know those old stories about Heaven or Hell?

Once upon a time, there was this real big businessman who died. He was very successful. And after he died he arrived at some gates. He saw this man, presumably the gatekeeper, and he said, "Peter, on Earth I was used to having a large car—a Cadillac—I want to go in and see what's here, where I'm going to be staying. Can I have a Cadillac?"

The gatekeeper said, "Why certainly, just think of it, and you've got it." So, he thought of a car, and rode around awhile, and came back, and said, "Well, Peter, I picked out the place where I want to live. Now, I had a pretty good house when I was on Earth—but it looks like, possibly, I can have an even better one here."

The gatekeeper said, "Certainly, all you have to do is see it, visualize it, and you have it, exactly what you want." He did and stayed there for quite a while. But he came back one day and said, "Peter, there's something wrong here. There's nothing going on. Nothing's happening. I never imagined that Heaven would be like this."

The gatekeeper said, "My friend, who said you were in Heaven?"

Just after death, there's a period of unconsciousness which may be likened to the dream state in the physical from which there is a gradual awakening. The duration of this period is governed by the individual's development.

In a reading on February 14, 1924, at the Phillips Hotel in Dayton, Ohio, for Arthur Lammers and others, Cayce said:

"In all thy getting, my son, get understanding." [Prov. 4:7] That of Self. When one understands self, and self's relation to its Maker, the duty to its neighbor, its own duty to self, it cannot, it will not be false to man, or to its Maker. Give then more thought, *for thoughts are deeds,* and are children of the relation

reached between the mental and the soul, and has
its relation to spirit and soul's plane of existence, as
they do in the physical or earth plane. What one
thinks continually, they become; what one cher-
ishes in their heart and mind they make a part of
the pulsation of their heart, through their own
blood cells, and build in their own physical, that
which its spirit and soul must feed upon, and that
with which it will be possessed, when it passes into
the realm for which the other experiences of what it
has gained here in the physical plane, must be used.
3744-5

In a reading on August 26, 1936, at Virginia Beach, for
a woman, fifty-five:

For mind is the builder and that which we think
upon may become crimes or miracles. For thoughts
are things and as their currents run through the environs of an entity's experience these become barriers or stepping-stones, dependent upon the manner
in which these are laid as it were. For *as* the mental
dwells upon these thoughts, so does it give strength,
power to things that do not appear. 906-3

In other words: What you constantly hold in your consciousness; what you hold in your mind; what you think
about—this you deal with during life, and you will deal
with at the point of death. Not someone else—but you!
At a reading in Rye, New York, on November 29, 1941,
Edgar Cayce told an actress and drama teacher, fifty-two,
Catholic:

Thus the outcome of any development, any
retardment, is according to the use the entity makes

of opportunities, and the ideal with which the entity entertains those opportunities. 2630-1

In a reading on January 15, 1925, in New York City, Morton Bumenthal asked:

> (Q) What form does the spirit entity take . . .
> (A) Taking that form that the entity creates for itself in the plane in which the existence is passed. As we have in the earth's plane the imagination, the mind of the individual pictures to itself, through its carnal relations, that condition to which its individual relation of the entity assumes to itself, and the entity possessing that same ability to assume that position in which it may manifest itself according to its relative position to that merited condition in its existence. 900-19

That's a complicated statement, but he's saying the same thing: What we think, we become. We think, and then we deal with it when we die.

In a reading on "Spirit Communication," given on March 17, 1927, at Virginia Beach, for Morton Blumenthal, Cayce said:

> In the make-up of the active forces of the physical body, it (the body) is constituted of many, many, cells—each with its individual world within itself, controlled by the spirit that is everlasting, and guided by that of the soul, which is a counterpart—or the breath that makes that body individual, and when the body is changed, and this is the soul body, the elements as are patterned are of the same. That is, that builded by thought and deed becomes the active particles, atoms, that make up that soul body, see?

When the soul passes, then, from the physical body, it (the soul body) then constituted with those atoms of thought (that are mind) and are of the Creative Forces a part, and then we have the soul body, with the mind, the subconscious mind, its attributes . . . which never forgets, and is then as the sensuous [conscious] mind of the soul body; the spirit or superconscious mind being that as the subconscious mind of the material body—the place, then, of the resident or residence, or that occupied by the soul body becomes to the finite mind the first question. The occupancy is at once—as is seen here, there are about us many, *many,* many, soul bodies; those upon whom the thought of an individual, the whole being of an individual is attracted to, by that element of thought—just the same as the action in the material body—for remember, we are patterned, see? one as of another. In the next, then, we find that, that as *builded* by that soul is as the residence of that soul, the companion with that as has been builded by that soul—either of the earth-bound or of that element or sphere, or plane, that has its attraction through that created in that soul being in the actions, by the thoughts, of that as an individual. Hence we find there are presented the same conditions in the astral or cosmic world, or cosmic consciousness, as is present in the material plane—until the consciousness of that soul has reached that development wherein such a soul is raised to that consciousness *above* the earth's sphere, or earth's attractive forces—until it reaches up, up, outward, until included in the *all,* see? 5756-4

Later in the same reading he was asked:

(Q) What form of consciousness does the spirit entity assume?

(A) That of the subconscious consciousness, as known in the material plane, or the acts and deeds, and thoughts, done in the body, are ever present before that being. Then consider what a hell digged by some, and what a haven and heaven builded by many. 5756-4

In another reading that same day in New York City, Morton Blumenthal asked:

(Q) Are the desires of the earth's plane carried over into the spiritual plane?

(A) When those desires have fastened such hold upon the inner being as to become a portion of the subconsciousness, those desires pass on. Such as one may have in gluttonousness, or in any condition that benumbs the mental forces of the entity, for the subconscious, as given, is the storehouse of every act, thought, or deed. Hence, as we have been given, all are weighed in the balance, as was given in . . . [quotation in Latin]. In these conditions, we find these conditions become a portion of the entity to the extent that the entirety of the subconscious becomes imbibed with that condition, wherein the entity depends upon that element for its sustenance. In such conditions these are carried over. Hence the condition as is seen about such entity having passed into the spirit plane, [it] seeks the gratification of such through the low minded individuals in an earth plane, for as thoughts become deeds, and as such desire is loosed in the plane, such conditions become the taking on of the entity from the sphere, as is given, in that "thoughts are deeds" and live as such. 900-20

In a dream reading on March 12, 1927, at Virginia
Beach, Morton Blumenthal, thirty-one, was told:

When the body physical lays aside the material
body, that in the physical called soul becomes the
body of the entity, and that called the superconscious
the consciousness of the entity, as the subconscious
is to the physical body. The subconscious [be-
comes] the mind or intellect of the body. 900-304

Or as the Buddha puts it:

The thought manifests as the word;
The word manifests as the deed;
The deed develops into habit;
And habit hardens into character;
So watch the thought and its ways with care,
And let it spring from love
Born out of concern for all beings . . .
As the shadow follows the body,
as we think, so we become.
                              From the Dhammapada
                              Sayings of the Buddha

10

Love

One day in the fall of 1926, Dad gave a reading for his mother Carrie, my grandmother, in Hopkinsville, Kentucky. His sister had written, asking Dad for a check reading. There was nothing specifically wrong with Carrie, except she was seventy, had had a little cold, but was up and about. Dad's sister wanted this checkup.

At the end of the reading, after the suggestion that he wake up, Dad said, "She is not seriously ill now, but if you [Edgar] want to see her alive, you should go to her immediately."

While he was a boy, Dad thought of his mom as his best friend, "the light of his life," until Mother came along. She was very dear to him. So he bought a train ticket to Hopkinsville and arrived at her house, where his mother, apparently in good health, met him at the front door. Yet here he was, showing up for her death, though he didn't mention it.

The next day she didn't want to get up. She wasn't suffering much, just felt weak. He sat and talked with her, and watched her gradually move out of her body, as he described it, then back in again. She talked with people on the other side—her mother, father, sister, all of whom had passed on. And Dad began to see these people coming and going. They were talking to Carrie, explaining what things were like "over there." And he began to hear what they were saying, or know what they were saying, rather than hear. They said they'd visit her during her transition. As Dad recounted it, she would get out of her body and talk to them, then get back in and talk to him. She was moving back and forth, in and out of her body, while Dad sat with her and alternately chatted and watched and listened. Once she said calmly, "Edgar, I'm going to die. I'm so glad you're here with me. I've been talking to Mom and Dad, and the next time they come, I'm going with them." She then told Dad what to do about his sisters and what else to do about this and that, as a mother would.

At the end of the second day, she died—quietly, peacefully, beautifully—as Dad described it, the kind of transition you'd like to engineer for yourself when the time comes.

There is a great deal in the Edgar Cayce readings that indicates that our loved ones are very close to us after death.

In a reading given on November 23, 1943, at Virginia Beach, a housewife, thirty-nine, whose brother had died, was told: "The entity has had the experience of awaking at night and feeling the presence of her brother—would appreciate an explanation of this."

This is a reality.

(Q) On June 2, 1942, the entity heard her brother calling her—was this the exact time that he passed on?

(A) Not the exact time, but when the entity could—and found the attunement such as to speak with thee.

(Q) Was there something he wanted her to know?

(A) Much that he needs of thee. Forget not to pray for and with him; not seeking to hold him but that he, too, may walk the way to the light, in and through the experience. For this is well. Those who have passed on need the prayers of those who live aright. For the prayers of those who would be righteous in spirit may save many who have erred, even in the flesh. 3416-1

In a reading on July 9, 1934, at Virginia Beach, volunteered at the end of a physical reading for a relative of Gertrude's, Edgar Cayce relayed a message for Gladys Davis:

Tell Tiny not to be so severe with 'Cille, else she will have a greater problem on her hands than has been in the last few weeks. Burt can handle it much better.

[Gladys Davis's note: My teenage sister, 'Cille, was living with my married sister, Tiny. My father picked up the friction and problems involved, and the correct solution. My brother Burt did step in and assume responsibility for my sister 'Cille. Mr. Cayce consciously did not know of the situation, nor did I.]

(Q) Who is this speaking?

(A) *Thomas* Davis! [Gladys Davis's father, Thomas Jefferson Davis] 5756-13

In a reading on July 17, 1934, at Virginia Beach, Gladys Davis asked for an explanation:

(Q) Gladys desires to know how her father [Thomas Jefferson Davis] came through with a message at that time.
(A) His anxiety! The anxiety of individuals, and their soul, respecting their loved ones. *Love* goes far beyond what ye have called the grave. The confusion that was being caused there over those particular influences that are making for such activities and changes in the lives of those that surround this home, in this particular period, brought it about. The channel open, the message came through. 5756-14

Note the phrase: "*Love* goes far beyond what ye have called the grave."
In a reading on February 15, 1926, at Virginia Beach, after the death of her mother, Mrs. Morton Blumenthal asked:

(Q) Night of Saturday, February 13, or Sunday morning, February 14, 1926. "I heard a voice that I recognized as J. S.'s, our old friend from New Orleans, who loved me dearly as a child, yet whom I have not seen in 2 to 3 years. The impression of J. S. talking to me was very pronounced, and for a while I did not see her figure, yet I felt that she was with Mother at the hospital, as mother changed from this earthly consciousness to the other. J. S. was there as the transition was made—was now with

Mother as she said to me: *'Your mother is as happy as ever.'''* More J. S. told me about Mother which I can't remember. Recall and explain to me, please.

(A) In this there is given to the entity that understanding of what is meant by the life other than the physical. For, as it is seen that the companionship of loved ones seek the companionship in that plane, for "As a tree falls so shall it lie," there is seen the message coming from the loved one to the one regarding the loved one, showing then that companionship, that without the loss of the care of others, as is seen.

Then, the entity should gain that strength from that given regarding the condition, and know that the mother lives in that realm in which there is recognized J. S., and that the companionship is there, until those developments come from the earth plane to lead on to those higher realms, or to come again. For those many changes must come to each and every entity in its development. And as these are seen, then, the strength, the understanding, should be gained by this entity. For as is given, she is *well, happy,* and *free* from the care as is given in earth's plane, yet with that same love as is raised through the companionship with the oneness of the spiritual forces with the soul, see . . .

(Q) Was J. S. there to guide Mother over the transition from physical to spiritual? Both died within 3 weeks—both must easily have yet been—be in this plane as yet—is this so?

(A) Both in physical plane or earth's sphere as yet, until that force leads on in its ever developing toward that Oneness with the All Force, see?

(Q) Then, does one spirit guide another over?

(A) "Lo! I am with thee, and though I walk through

the valley of the shadow of death, my spirit shall guide thee." As is seen in this, these are given in this manner that those may see, those may know, through that experience of such earthly partings, that is the lack of an understanding of that spiritual consciousness that prevents these forces from manifesting in the physical sense.

(Q) Voice: "Your Mother is alive and happy."

(A) Your mother is alive and happy. Just as is given, the entity may know that all force goes to show, to prove, to bring to the consciousness of the entity, that through that as ye *live* in Him ye shall be made *alive* in Him! for there is no death, only the transition from the physical to the spiritual plane. Then, as the birth into the physical is given as the time of the new life, just so, then, in physical is the birth into the spiritual.

(Q) Then, does my mother see me and love me as ever?

(A) Sees thee and loves thee as ever. Just as those forces were manifest in the physical world, and the entity entertains and desires and places self in that attunement with those desires of that entity, the love exists, in that far, in that manner, see? for in spirit all sham is laid aside.

(Q) Does she try to tell me "I am alive and happy"?

(A) *Tells* the entity "I am alive and happy" when entity will *attune* self to that at-oneness. 136-33

In a reading on January 4, 1926, at Virginia Beach, for Mrs. Edwin Blumenthal, twenty-three:

(Q) [After I pass on,] could I deliver a message to ... my mother? Then why could not I deliver a message through another mind, another channel that I might find, to convey a message to Edwin?

(A) Only with an attunement is the message received, as in the radio. Only with the same attunement may a message be delivered to an individual, see? . . . the medium is as but that through which the transmission of a condition passes or exists, and is wavered by that physical, by that cosmic consciousness of that individual; while (get the difference, see?) a subconscious condition in which the subconscious contacts by suggestion the whole one spirit force that is, as an element of existent force in nature, and in the condition, the presentation of the fact—is manifested according to abilities of the entity to present same to the consciousness of the individual desiring that information from that cosmic consciousness, see? You don't see, but this is it, see? 140-10

In another reading for Mrs. Edwin Blumenthal, twenty-five, on October 31, 1927, at Virginia Beach, she sought interpretation of a dream of a dead friend:

(Q) Of recent date. A communication with Louis Schoolhouse in which I said: "If you really are Louis Schoolhouse, pull me by the side." I felt myself pulled by the side in no uncertain manner and jumping up [I] screamed in fear.

(A) Here we have that full demonstration of the action of the subconscious forces when the consciousness is in subjugation or abeyance to the subconscious forces, and the illustration that the subconscious is in such condition—attunement to the cosmic or ethereal plane upon which such a one as Louis Schoolhouse is, and that such communi-

cation is of that nature so that, would the body consciousness not so fear—or that condition wherein
this condition is out of attunement—the full meaning may be given to the body; that this condition,
this communication, this illustration, is *not* to be
dreaded, not to be made the whole of the mind's
experience; not to be looked upon other than the
natural consequences of conditions. For, will this be
looked upon in this manner, there may again come
to the body such an experience that will satisfy the
body of that that the soul of that individual *is* as an
individual, and conscious of that that is in the material as well as that place, position, condition, occupied by the spirit or soul in the cosmic forces, see?
Such an experience may come to the entity, will the
entity allow self to be attuned to such conditions.
Will fear and the wish *not* to be made aware of such
conditions be held in the will of the *entity,* as the
whole, such conditions may not penetrate to the
consciousness of the body in a way and manner
that the physical body may be aware of such conditions. 140-18

11

The Inter-Between

The following extract reminds one of the layperson's concept of purgatory. Notice the idea of a soul meriting a certain state of consciousness after death. In a reading on Dad's dreams, January 13, 1925, at the Cambridge Hotel in New York City, Edgar Cayce was asked:

(Q) Where do entities recede to after leaving earth's plane?

(A) . . . In the separation of the soul and spirit from an earthly abode, each enter the spirit realm. When the entity has fully completed its separation, it goes to that force through which the entity merits in the action upon the earth's plane, and in the various spheres, or in the various elements, as has been prepared for its (the spiritual entity) development, so the sojourn is taken, until the entity is ready for again manifesting through the flesh that development attained in the spiritual entity, for the will *must* be made one with the Father, that we may enter into that realm of the blessed, for, as has been given [Matthew 5:8], only the true, the perfect, may see God [Hebrews 12:14], and we *must* be one with Him. 294-15

On August 6, 1933, at Virginia Beach, in a reading on Jesus, Minnie Barrett asked:

(Q) Is the Celestial Sphere a definite place in the Universe or is it a state of mind?
(A) When an entity, a soul, passes into any sphere, with that it has builded in its celestial body, it must occupy—to a finite mind—space, place, time. Hence, to a finite mind, a body can only be in a place, a position. An attitude, sure—for that of a onement with, or attunement with, the Whole.
For, God is love; hence occupies a space, place, condition, and *is* the Force that permeates all activity. 5749-4

In a reading on December 31, 1924, at Dayton, Ohio, Morton Blumenthal asked:

(Q) Does the spiritual entity, after leaving this earth's plane, have full realization of the physical life, or experience through which it passed while on earth's plane?
(A) It may, should it so choose. As has been given. As in this: In the way that the spiritual insight was

given into the heart and soul of Saul of Tarsus, as he beheld his Master in that realm to which he had passed. The consciousness in the material world, through the material consciousness of another material individual. The vision as beheld by him, in the way that of the superconscious manifests in his subconsciousness.

(Q) . . . Will that full realization remain with him in the next plane, or when he leaves this earth's sphere? Will he know he was [Morton Blumenthal] on earth, an individual with definite personality and character, and will he be able to realize that which he was and that which he has become?

(A) When he, [Morton Blumenthal], has reached that perfect realization of these consciousnesses of personae and personalities of individuals, and of self, (to which he may develop) he will become able to attain such superconsciousness in a spiritual plane, as has been outlined. At present, no. 900-16

In a reading on March 6, 1929, at Virginia Beach, Morton Blumenthal, thirty-three, asked:

(Q) [Is it true] that the memory reveals itself sometime after death to a spiritual minded person, not only as related to the earthy life, or the remaining earthly thoughts *of* earthly life, but *also* reveals itself as a self unfoldment of *all* past experiences.

(A) Correct. For life, in its continuity, is that experience of the soul or entity—including its soul, its spirit, its superconscious, its subconscious, its physical consciousness, or its *material* consciousness, in that as its *development* goes through the various experiences takes on more and more [of] that ability of knowing itself to be itself, yet a por-

tion of the great whole, or the one Creative Energy
that is in and through all. 900-426

Next we find the idea that a soul on the next plane of
consciousness first takes on and then moves out of a
bodylike form as it progresses in its spiritual evolution.
Students of Theosophy will find parallel concepts here.
Notice that this answers a question about astral projection.

In a reading on September 13, 1935, at Virginia Beach,
a club woman, fifty-seven, Spiritualist, asked:

(Q) In regard to my first projection of myself into
the astral plane, about two weeks ago: Some of the
people were animated and some seemed like waxen
images of themselves. What made the difference?

(A) Some—those that appear as images—are the
expressions or shells or the body of an individual
that has been left when its soul self has projected
on, and has not been as yet dissolved—as it were—
to the realm of that activity.

For what individuals are lives on and takes form
in that termed by others as the astral body. The soul
leaves same, and it appears as seen. Other individuals, as experienced, are in their *animated* form
through their own sphere of experience at the
present.

(Q) Why did I see my father and his two brothers
as young men, although I knew them when they
were white-haired?

(A) They are growing, as it were, upon the eternal
plane. For, as may be experienced in every entity, a
death is a birth. And those that are growing then
appear in their growing state.

(Q) Any other advice?

(A) First, do those things that will make thine body—as it were—*whole.* Projections, inflections, astral experiences, are much harder upon those who are not *wholly* physically fit. 516-4

In a reading on March 13, 1933, at Norfolk, Virginia, for the Prayer Group and others studying the Book of Revelation, Edgar Cayce said:

The passing in, the passing out, is as but the summer, the fall, the spring; the birth into the interim, the birth into the material. 281-16

A reading on March 17, 1927, at Virginia Beach for Edgar Cayce and Morton Blumenthal stated:

The growth in the astral world is the growth, or the digesting and the building of that same oneness in the spirit, the conscious, the subconscious, the cosmic, or the astral world. 5756-4

12

Soul Communication

For a moment, let's return to Dad's dream of himself as a dot, following a shaft of light through planes of darkness, past grotesque figures on either side, magnified parts of human bodies. And on through to a static place, much like the earth, but static—nothing moving; nothing happening. To a place where there was laughter, color, noise, movement, growth—where things were changing, developing. Then, beyond that, to another place of just sound, then sound and color together. Then to a Hall of Records. And beyond that, a few times, to a place where there were schools, reading, and work. A dream of the planes of consciousness.

Other psychic sources have reported levels and planes

we travel to during sleep.

While returning to consciousness, my father would, apparently, stop and talk to certain people. He didn't do this often, just now and then. Some examples follow.

After a check physical reading on July 9, 1934, following the suggestion for Edgar Cayce to awaken, he began an extemporaneous discourse. Gertrude Cayce, Gladys and Mildred Davis, and L.B. Cayce were present. This occurred during the regular schedule of appointed readings:

Mr. Cayce: There are some here that would speak with those that are present, if they desire to so communicate with them.

Mrs. Cayce: We desire to have at this time that which would be given.

Mr. Cayce: [Long pause] Don't all speak at once. [pause] Yes. I knew you would be waiting, though. Yes? Haven't found him before? All together then now, huh? Uncle Porter, too? He was able to ease it right away, huh? *Who?* Dr. House? No. Oh, no. No, she is all right. Yes, *lots* better. Isn't giving any trouble now. Haven't seen her? Why? Where have you been? Oh. She is in another change? How long will they stay there? Oh, they don't count time like that. Oh, you do have 'em. Well, those must be pretty now, if they are all growing like that way. Yes? Yes, I'll tell her about 'em. Tell Gertrude you are all together now, huh? Uncle Porter, Dr. House, your mother? And Grandma. Oh. Grandpa still building. Oh, he made the house; yeah. Tell Tommy what? *Yes!* Lynn? Yes, he's at home. Oh, you knew that! Huh? Ain't any difference? Well, how about the weather? Oh, the weather don't affect you now. Don't change. Oh, you have what you want to—depends on where you go. Sure, then you are subject to that anyway. Little baby too! How big is it? Oh, he is *grown* now, huh? Yes. Coming back! When? Oh. Uhhuh. All right. Why? Oh yes, they hear you—I'm sure they do. I hear you! For Gertrude? Yes, she is here—she hears you. Oh, yes!

Mrs. Cayce: I don't hear. May I have the message?

Mr. Cayce: Sure, she hears you; don't you hear her talking? No, I don't know what she says.

Mrs. Cayce: I don't hear. Will you repeat the message for me?

Mr. Cayce: Mama and Dr. House and Uncle Porter and the baby—we are all here. Grandpa has built the home here, and it's *nice!* And we are all waiting until you come, and we will all be here ready—we are getting along *fine,* doing *well,* yes! No. No more troubles now, for spring borders [?] all along the way; for we have reached together where we see the light and know the pathway to the Savior is along the narrow way that leads to *His* throne. We are on that plane where you have heard it spoken of that the body, the mind, are one with those things we have builded. Yes, I still play baseball, and Charlie has recently joined my club and I am still Captain to many of 'em. Well, we will be waiting for you! 5756-13

When asked who gave this information, Edgar Cayce said, "Hugh," which would have been Hugh Evans, Gertrude's younger brother, who died many years before.

Only a few examples of this type of communication are found in the records; however, they reveal a great deal about life after death, as Dad knew it through his readings.

We sense a movement on the part of Edgar Cayce's mind. For example: "I knew you would be waiting," "Where have you been?" " . . . they don't count time like that," " . . . all along the way." Evidently, while returning from his reading attunement, he paused. He may have recognized friends and begun chatting. Those present could hear only one side of this conversation as he repeated specific messages.

Interesting that Gertrude's brother reported a physical activity he'd enjoyed on earth ("I still play baseball"). He died of tuberculosis and had given up the game during his last years. He also speaks of a home being finished by the grandfather. This home had become a symbol of family stability—a "point of return" for family members in time of trouble. The grandfather was building it when he died; it was enlarged during the brother's lifetime, but not completed. The desire of the grandfather was apparently fulfilled in the afterlife, when his family was with him.

Notice that the young man had begun to recognize this home as a place on a path, rather than "heaven." Notice references to the weather and a nonlinear measurement of time. The people mentioned all died at different intervals. The "baby" was probably Milton Porter Cayce, my brother, a son of Edgar and Gertrude's who died as an infant. In Gertrude's brother's mind at least, growth had continued. Does "coming back" refer to reincarnation? The young man didn't believe in rebirth when he died.

More information was obtained on this in another reading on July 17, 1934:

Mrs. Cayce: You will have before you the body and enquiring mind of Edgar Cayce and all present in this room, in regard to the experience following the reading Monday afternoon, July 9, 1934; explaining to us what happened—and why—at that particular time, answering the questions that may be asked.

Mr. Cayce: Yes, we have the body, the enquiring mind, Edgar Cayce, and those present in this room, together with the experience had by all present in the room on July 9, 1934.

In giving that which may be helpful, for the moment turn to that known by the body of self and by those present in the room respecting what is ordinarily termed spirit communication—should be (and that which has caused much of the dissension)—*soul* communication. For the soul lives on; and as conditions are only the release of the soul body from a house of clay the activities in the world of matter are only changed in their *relationships* to that which produces same and that the physical body sees in material or three-dimensional form. For words are the combination of sound. Sound is an activity of those things that produce or bring vibrations to activity to be heard, and are communicable to those of the various attunements.

Here we find, in the experience, that there were those that were in attune—through the vibrations from that sounded in the room at that particular period—and these sought, many—even many that spoke not, to communicate of themselves that there might be known not only their continued existence in a world of matter but of finer matter. As the sound of that attuned to those of the various vibrations are of its tonal or active force, it brings the variations in same—and they sought through those channels through which the soul-force of the body was passing at the particular time to produce that which would make known their presence in activity in that particular period; that although the various communications given at the time were from those thought to be dead (from the physical viewpoint) or in other realms, yet their souls, their personalities, their individualities, live on; the personalities being lost gradually in the oneness of the purpose and desire towards things that are the continual activity in a realm of whatever has been meted or measured by that builded in the individual experience. Hence communicated, as heard, through the soul forces of the body Edgar Cayce in its accord to those individualities that were attempting to make known their realm of activity in their various spheres of experiences at the time. See? Ready for questions.

(Q) Why did we only hear one side of the conversation?

(A) Denseness of matter to the spirit realm. All felt the presence of these influences, that attuned themselves to those activities. Spoke He, the Master, "They that have ears to hear, let them hear." There be none so deaf as those who do not want to hear. All could hear if they would attune themselves to the realm of the activity during such an experience.

How (some would ask) did the body, Edgar Cayce, or soul, attune self at that particular period and yet not remember in the physical consciousness that conversation had with those that approached to communicate or to tell those things that were to them, are to them, very vital in their experiences in the present plane? This, as has been given, is because the soul passes from the body into those realms from which is sought that desired to be known by the seeker. Here there was sought (this is

on the 9th of July, see?) concerning the physical
condition of a body that which in the material world
would aid in correcting the mental and physical
conditions. This realm from which such information is obtainable, as we have given, is either from
those that have passed into the realm of subconscious activity or from the subconscious and superconscious activity through which information is
being sought by that superconscious activity in the
realm of physical forces in action. Hence why this
particular body, Edgar Cayce, was able to attune self
to the varied realms of activity by laying aside the
physical consciousness. 5756-14

This was followed by a summary of what had just been
given and comments about other family members. The
entire reading gives insight into what Cayce meant by
"movement in consciousness" and "attunement."
Here is another example:
At Virginia Beach, on May 6, 1929, two readings had
been given for men in distant cities. Gertrude had given
the suggestion for Edgar to wake up, when Edgar, in his
normal voice, as always, gave this strange discourse:

Here, Sister—before you change this, let me give
you a little piece of advice concerning what you are
working with. As there are many questions often
asked you, and as you often feel others are not as
considerate of the position you occupy with the
Forces as are manifested through Cayce, these are
the things that will possibly aid you in understanding just what takes place, and as to how you—personally—may assist or may aid the individual
seeking to know that as may be helpful, beneficial
to themselves or their loved ones, or where others

seek to gain for themselves that same experience of the position you, yourself, now occupy in obtaining for others or for self such information.

This is the condition that is ever present when such information is obtained:

When the consciousness is laid aside, there is that which takes place much in the same manner as the spring to an automatic curtain roller. This, then, is able to be pulled down or raised up with the release of the spring. *Some* call this going into the unknown. *Some* call this spiritual, or spirit, communication. Some call it the ability to gain the force of the activities of the fourth dimension—which is *nearer* correct than any explanation that may be given. For it is the plane that is of the inter-between, or that of the borderland—which all individuals occupy through that period of gaining consciousness of that sphere they themselves occupy, until such a period or such a time that there is that joining together of such forces as may again bring that individual entity into the realm of physical experience or being.

Now each individual seeks experiences, see? Each individual must experience conditions to become aware of that being present or existent in their *own* experience, or that becomes a portion of the whole of that entity.

Then, know, whenever there is the wholehearted desire of all seeking such, there may be the perfect action of the roller or spring, or there may be the perfect application of the information that may be gained.

But Sister, know this—whenever you, yourself, are in the position of the question[er], or the one seeking to gain for another such information, call

me—I will answer. This is Gay. We are through.
538-28

By way of background, I should note that Dr. Samuel
G. Gay of Selma, Alabama, had been our family physician. He took care of me when I burned my eyes, operated on Dad for appendicitis, and delivered my brother
Edgar Evans. Dr. Gay died while we were in Selma. His
nickname for Mom was "Sister."
This appears to be a direct telepathic communication.
Edgar Cayce is not talking with Gay; rather, Gay's
thoughts appear to be acting directly through Cayce's
subconscious. It seems possible that Edgar Cayce had
moved to Gay's plane of consciousness for direct contact, rather than that Gay had moved to Cayce's level of
consciousness. Gay explains the readings as "activities
of the fourth dimension."
Notice that Gay says, "again bring that individual entity into the realm of physical experience," a seeming reference to rebirth. He was not known to have accepted
reincarnation while alive; neither had Edgar Cayce,
while Gay was alive. This did not come up until the life
readings began in Dayton, Ohio, 1923, years after Gay
died. Here, then, is a communication dealing with ideas
which were not part of an entity's thought processes at
death.
Gay seems aware of at least some of Gertrude's
thought patterns, a phenomenon that could have origi-
nated in Edgar Cayce's subconscious and masqueraded
as Gay. What is curious, however, is Gay's last remark:
" . . . whenever you, yourself, are in the position of the
question[er]." When Gay knew the Cayces, various
people acted as reading conductors. At the time of this
reading, however, Gertrude conducted practically all the
readings. Time, at least for Dr. Gay, seems out of focus.

Here's another unsolicited communication in the readings, given at Edgar Cayce's office, 115 West 35th St., Virginia Beach, after two check-physical readings, April 10, 1929:

Now, there are many here that would speak concerning the various things as has been given regarding the educational end of the institutional work. *Three* would speak concerning the varied approach, of the way as is given by each.

As we find, Robertson would say—In the presentation of the pamphlets as lessons, the spectacular of each individual experience is an approach.

While we find Funk would say—The *reason* and the self-application would be the better approach.

While we find, as is presented by Hudson—that the *way* of individual approach is the manner that should be presented in *any* information as is given to the public, knowing that—as has so often been said—it is first to the individual, *then* to the classes, then to the masses. *Classes* being the classification under the three heads as may be presented under the teaching or the *influence* of each of these who were teachers in their physical experience. One the wonderer, the other the student, the other the reasoner—or the exhorter. In each field there is a class. While individuals differ, let the first *principle* be the starting point—*all is one!* We are through for the present. 5756-7

In discussing the information after the reading, we concluded that Edgar Cayce was referring to Morgan Robertson, American writer of sea tales who sought information on sunken treasure; Dr. I. K. Funk, world traveler, cofounder of Funk & Wagnalls dictionary firm; and

Dr. Thomson Jay Hudson, author of *The Law of Psychic Phenomena.*

Here the communication is through ideas, but there is also a definite reference to personalities existing on some plane of consciousness. Possibly, in moving through various levels, Edgar Cayce ran into thought-forms representing attitudes held by these men and the relationship of these attitudes toward proposed activities.

13

Prayers for the Dead

In a reading on August 7, 1932, at Virginia Beach, while Search for God Group #1 was writing the lesson, "Patience," Ruth LeNoir said:

> (Q) From time to time I have had to come into my room a friend who has passed on. Is this contact harmful or beneficial?
> (A) In this, there are always those seeking that we may help, that may help us; for as we help another does help come to us. Pray for that friend, that the way through the shadows may be easier for them. It becomes easier for you. 262-25

In a reading on November 5, 1943, at Virginia Beach, for a woman, seventy-one, Edgar Cayce said:

Yea, pray oft for those who have passed on. This is part of thy consciousness. It is well. For, God is God of the living. Those who have passed through God's other door are oft listening, listening for the voice of those they have loved in the earth. The nearest and dearest thing they have been conscious of in earthly consciousness. And the prayers of others that are still in the earth may ascend to the throne of God, and the angel of each entity stands before the throne to make intercession. Not as a physical throne, no; but that consciousness in which we may be so attuned that we become one with the whole in lending power and strength to each entity for whom ye speak and pray.

For, where two or three are gathered together in His name, He is in the midst of them. What meaneth this? If one be absent from the body, He is present with His Lord. What Lord? If you have been the ideal, that one to whom another would pay homage, you are then something of the channel, of the ideal. Then thy prayers direct such an one closer to that throne of love and mercy, that pool of light, yea that river of God. 3954-1

In a reading on July 22, 1930, at Virginia Beach, for a woman, fifty-two, Edgar Cayce was asked:

(Q) Is there any message you could give regarding her husband, who has passed beyond, that would help her?
(A) These, as we may find, may best be had

through that introspection of self in those periods when one may turn to the within and seek that counsel, that at-oneness with those who are in the borderland; for *all* is well in the oneness of the purposes as may be accomplished in this material force through the mental changing, or guiding, that the *spirit* may work aright. 5488-1

In a life reading on June 15, 1940, at Virginia Beach, for a woman, fifty-seven, Christian Scientist, Edgar Cayce was asked:

(Q) Please explain why I have had to experience the loss of my two sons, during the last few years.

(A) As in those experiences when ye gained the greater knowledge of truth, light, understanding, ye experienced and saw many a mother, many a home lose hope, lose help, lose all, ye are meeting this in thy own experience.

Let it be rather that as would draw thee nearer, nearer; for Life is a continuous thing. For, as given, it is a manifestation of that we would call God . . .

And in thy patience ye will become aware of thy soul. And by thy activities with thy fellow men ye may draw nearer and nearer to the using of that in those ways and manners that endear that suffering in Him—who is the way, the truth and the light.

(Q) Can you tell me if my older son, who passed away last May, died of natural causes or was he killed?

(A) An accident.

(Q) Can I be of any help to my sons now? If so, how?

(A) Prayer for those who are seeking a way, *the* way to the light, aids ever.

As ye meditate—as ye pray—for as thy body is
indeed the temple of the living God, there He hath
promised to meet thee—then as ye meet Him, thy
Maker, thy Lord—pray that there may be the light,
the help needed, that they may be guided in that
way and manner which will bring all together in the
way as *He*, thy Lord, would have it. 2280-1

In a mental and spiritual reading on January 13, 1944,
at Virginia Beach, for an engineer, forty-three, Christian
Scientist, Edgar Cayce was asked:

(Q) Regarding my brother [2564] (who passed
from the earth life about eighteen months ago), is it
indicated that he is happy?
(A) As was his purpose, so is the activity. As indicated through the experience given thee in His
word, pray for and with him if ye would help.
2524-5

In a reading on July 20, 1932, at Virginia Beach, for the
Prayer and Healing Group, Edgar Cayce was asked if one
member's husband, who died of cancer, was aided by
healing prayers. Edgar Cayce replied:

Still gaining from same!
(Q) Can we help him further?
(A) If he is still gaining, you can still help him!
281-8

In a reading on October 28, 1935, at the David Kahn
home in New York City, Edgar Cayce was asked about a
girl, eighteen, who fell out of a dormitory window at
Barnard College in New York City and was killed. He responded:

Yes, we are with the entity here.

This, as may be and should be understood by those who are interested, was an accident—and not premeditated or purposed by the entity.

The environs or surroundings that made for these happenings, in a material world, are with the entity in the present, making for better understandings.

Those that are near and dear to the entity, to make for more understandings—condemn no one, nor the circumstance. Neither mourn for those that are at rest.

There is gradually coming the awakening. This, to be sure, is an experience through which the entity, [4938], is passing in the present. It is making for a helpfulness in its understanding and comprehending of that which is the experience, the awareness of same in the present.

The body-physical that was broken is now whole in Him . . .

(Q) Is she happy, and does she understand where she is?

(A) As given, there is the awakening, and there is the understanding coming more and more.

And soon to the Aunt may come the awareness of her presence near.

These are the conditions.

(Q) Is there anything any of us can do to help her in any way?

(A) Let the prayer . . . be held occasionally, especially in the early mornings. 4938-1

14

Edgar Cayce's Sources

Many people are sincerely concerned with the ethics and advisability of communication in spirit realms—the possible harm or benefit to those in the material and other planes. Is it right to communicate? Is it helpful to those with whom we communicate? Should we make the attempt, and if so, how? And what kinds of communication are there?

The readings themselves had a lot to say on that subject, but first let's talk about Edgar Cayce's sources. Where was he getting the information for the many documented diagnoses, prescriptions, and healings that occurred in the readings?

Students of psychical research, especially those involved with spiritualism, assume that Edgar Cayce acted as a medium. I've often been asked: "Who was Edgar Cayce's guide?" a question which assumes a group of doctors were helping him.

This differs markedly from what the readings themselves claimed. The readings said that Cayce could communicate with entities on other planes, but was not limited to them. If this is true, those who act as mediums for discarnate spirits might be limiting themselves by not recognizing their own latent soul powers, powers we've forgotten, Cayce says, and are our God-given heritage since the creation of humankind.

In a reading on October 8, 1937, at Virginia Beach, a woman, twenty-nine, Christian, was told:

> For a man is a little lower than the angels, yet was made that he might become the companion of the Creative Forces; and thus was given—in the breath of life—the individual soul, the stamp of approval as it were of the Creator; with the ability to know itself to be itself, and to make itself, as one with the Creative Forces—*irrespective* of other influences. 1456-1

In a reading for a divorced man, forty-six, Protestant, on April 19, 1940, in Bronxville, N.Y., Edgar Cayce said:

> Yet, know that no urge, no sign, no emotion— whether of a latent mental nature or of a material or emotional nature finding expression in the body—surpasses that birthright, *will*—the factor which makes the human soul, the human individual, *different* from all other creatures in the earth, from all manifestations of God's activity!

For he, man, has been made just a little lower
than the angels; with all the abilities to become *one
with him!* not the whole, nor yet lost in the individuality of the whole, but becoming more and more
personal in *all* of its consciousnesses of the application of the individuality of Creative Forces, thus
more and more at-onement with Him—yet conscious of being himself. 2172-1

In a life reading on May 30, 1938, at Virginia Beach, a
housewife, forty, of Catholic background was told that
she had been Eunice, a friend of Mary, the mother of the
Master. She asked:

(Q) Are the inspirational writings I receive to be
relied upon as coming from a worthy and high
source or should I not cultivate this form of guidance and information?
(A) We would *not* from here counsel *anyone* to be
guided by influences from without. For the *king-
dom* is from within!
If these come as inspirational writings from
within, and not as guidance from others—that is
different! 1602-1

In a previously quoted reading on February 3, 1934, at
the Zentgraf home on Staten Island, Mrs. Eileen Garrett,
medium for spirit guide, Uvani, asked:

(Q) If Edgar Cayce has ever had controls, does he
know who they are?
(A) Anyone may speak who may seek, if the entity or the soul's activities will allow same; or if the
desire of the individuals seeking so over commands
as to make for a set channel . . .

(Q) If Edgar Cayce goes into trance without any control, could he not in a waking state get the inspiration direct?

(A) Not until there has been a more perfect cleansing of the carnal influences in the experiences of the soul, as has been indicated. With the regeneration that should come into the experience of the entity, this then may be the manner, the channel, the way through which much of constructive forces may be given. 507-1

Those who had their own readings and those who listened regularly never observed evidence that "spirit entities" took over the body or voice of Edgar Cayce. His voice never changed in tone, timbre, or inflection during a reading. In volume—yes. But he never manifested a personality trait in his altered state that we didn't recognize as Edgar Cayce, the man himself, awake or asleep. We have letters from many who were disappointed when they found that a reading would not permit them to speak with loved ones in the "spirit world." So Edgar Cayce did not act as a medium in the usual sense.

Edgar Cayce's sources were described in a reading in Selma, Alabama, on March 19, 1919.

We have the body here [Edgar Cayce]—we have had it before. In this state the conscious mind is under subjugation of the subconscious or soul mind. The information obtained and given by this body is obtained through the power of mind over mind, or power of mind over physical matter, or obtained by the suggestion as given to the active part of the subconscious mind. It obtains its information from that which it has gathered, either from other subconscious minds—put in touch with the power of the suggestion of the mind controlling the speaking faculties of this body, or from minds that have passed into the Beyond, which leave their impressions and are brought in touch by the power of the suggestion. What is known to one subconscious mind or soul is known to another, whether conscious of the fact or not. The subjugation of the conscious mind putting the subconscious in action in this manner or in one of the other of the manners as described, this body obtains its information when in the subconscious state. 254-2

Dr. Wesley H. Ketchum, quoting from reading 294-1, described Edgar Cayce's psychic sources in a *New York Times* story on October 9, 1910:

Edgar Cayce's mind is amenable to suggestion, the same as all other subconscious minds, but in addition thereto it has the power to interpret to the objective mind of others what it acquires from the subconscious mind of other individuals of the same kind. The subconscious mind forgets nothing. The conscious mind receives the impression from without and transfers all thought to the subconscious, where it remains even though the conscious be destroyed. The subconscious mind of Edgar Cayce is in direct communication with all other subconscious minds, and is capable of interpreting through his objective mind and imparting impressions received to other objective minds, gathering in this way all knowledge possessed by millions of other subconscious minds.

Does this seem impossible? So also to most of us would seem the feats of a virtuoso pianist, an aerobatic pilot, or an Olympic diver. Yet, the readings say that Edgar Cayce developed his abilities the same way as would a pianist, a pilot, or a diver—by desire, will, and practice. The readings speak of "mental planes" beyond the earth.

In a reading on March 19, 1919, in Selma, Alabama, Cayce was asked:

(Q) Do the planets have anything to do with the ruling of the destiny of men? If so, what? and what do they have to do with this body?

(A) They do. In the beginning, as our own planet, Earth, was set in motion, the placing of other planets began the ruling of the destiny of all matter as created, just as the division of waters was and is ruled by the moon in its path about the Earth; just so as in the higher creation, as it began, is ruled by the action of the planets about the earth.

The strongest power in the destiny of man is the Sun, first; then the closer planets, or those that are coming in ascendency at the time of the birth of the individual; but let it be understood here, no action of any planet or any of the phases of the Sun, Moon, or any of the heavenly bodies surpass the rule of Man's individual will power—the power given by the Creator of man in the beginning, when he became a living soul, with the power of choosing for himself.

The inclination of man is ruled by the planets under which he is born. In this far the destiny of man lies within the sphere or scope of the planets. With the given position of the Solar system at the time of the birth of an individual, it can be worked out—that is, the inclinations and actions without the will power taken into consideration.

As in this body here [Edgar Cayce] born March 18, 1877, three minutes past three o'clock, with the Sun descending, on the wane, the Moon in the opposite side of the Earth (old moon), Uranus at its zenith, hence the body is ultra in its actions. Neptune closest in conjunction or Neptune as it is termed in Astrological survey, in the ninth house; Jupiter, the higher force of all the planets, save the Sun, in descendency, Venus just coming to horizon, Mars just set, Saturn—to whom all insufficient matter is cast at its decay—opposite the face of the Moon. Hence the inclination as the body is controlled by the Astrological survey at the time of the birth of this body, either (no middle ground for this body) very good or very bad, very religious or very wicked, very rich or always losing, very much in love or hate, very much given to good works or always doing wrong, governed entirely by the will of the body. Will is the educational factor of the body; thence the patience, the persistence, the ever faithful attention that should be given to the child when it is young.

As to the forces of this body, the psychical is obtained through action of Uranus and of Neptune, always it has been to this body and always will, just outside the action of firearms, yet ever within them, just saved financially and spiritually by the action of great amount of water—the body should live close to the sea, should always have done so. The body is strange to other bodies in all of its actions, in the psychical life, in all of its ideas as expressed in the spiritual life as to its position on all matter pertaining to political, religious or economical positions. This body will either be very rich or very poor.

(Q) Will this work hurt the body?

(A) Only through the action or power of suggestion over the body. This body is controlled in its work through the psychical or the mystic or the spiritual. It is governed by the life that is led by the person who is guiding the subconscious when in this state, or by the line of thought that is given to create ideas of expression to the subconscious.

As the ideas given the subconscious to obtain its information are good, the body becomes better; if bad or wicked it becomes under the same control. Then the body should not be held responsible save through the body controlling the body at such times. 254-2

Note the stress placed upon the conductor's ideals. Until Mom took over most of the readings in the 1920s, Dad was often led astray by the ideals and purposes of other conductors. Sometimes this caused distress, headaches, even the loss of his ability to give a reading. The reading continues:

(Q) Can this power be used to be of assistance to humanity and also to obtain financial gain?

(A) There are many channels through which information obtained from this body in this state would be of assistance to humanity. To obtain financial gain from these is to obtain that which is just and right to those dependent upon this body for the things of life. Not those that would be destructive to the bodies themselves, physically or mentally, but that which is theirs by right should be obtained for such information.

As to which is the best channel, it depends as to whether the information desired is in accord with

the ideas of the body from which they are attempting to obtain them.

When credence is given to the work in a material
way, anyone is willing to pay in a financial way for
such information; but without credence there can
be nothing obtained. 254-2

Finances were often a major concern for our family
and those who worked with Edgar Cayce. In a reading
for Vincent Lopez, thirty-five, musical conductor, on August 14, 1931, at the Hotel Victoria in New York City,
Edgar Cayce was asked:

(Q) Why don't the Forces prevent continual financial annoyance to him?

(A) That there has been set a monetary *standard*
by many as to that which is of worth or is success,
indicates the vibrations as well as the purpose of
such. Not by might nor by power, but by "My Word."
Not that man lives by bread alone, but by *every word*
that is a promise to that man by or from the Creative Forces, or God. That that a man worships, *that*
that man becomes.

(Q) What are the revelations as to why he is in difficulty?

(A) No difficulty exists in the man's soul. There
exists difficulty in the minds of individuals who,
with monetary *measures,* see all forces hindered as
to their concept of success. 2897-4

In a previously quoted reading for a stockbroker, forty-
six, on June 20, 1944, at Virginia Beach, Edgar Cayce said:

Do *not*, then, allow self to become so material-
minded that the judgments are measured only by

the material yardstick of material accomplishments. For what profiteth a man who does gain the whole world and loseth his own soul? Or what would ye gain in exchange for the awareness of thy soul, that ye may know life is indeed eternal; and it isn't then all of life to live, nor all of death to die. 3436-2

In the previously quoted reading, 254-2, on March 19, 1919, in Selma, Alabama, Cayce was asked:

(Q) Is there any other information that this body [Edgar Cayce] should have now?

(A) The body should keep close in touch with the spiritual side of life; with sincerity to the spiritual side of life, if he is to be successful, mentally, physically, psychically and financially.

The safest brace is in the spiritual nature of the body; sincerity of the work done or obtained through any channel with which this body is connected is governed by the masses through the action of the body towards the spiritual. 254-2

Note the phrase: "The safest brace is in the spiritual nature of the body . . . " (254-2)

That's why Dad focused on serving his family, friends, church, and community. That's why he spent so much time praying, reading his Bible, and working in his garden.

Other readings state that Edgar Cayce's talents and shortcomings were developed in past lives; indeed, that the talents and shortcomings of all of us have been developed in past lives, a concept we'll discuss later. But what about Edgar Cayce's ability to give a reading? Upon what did he focus to achieve the attunement necessary for him to see that flash of white light?

A reading's clarity, depth, range, and accuracy were affected by his pre-reading degree of attunement. Other factors were the need, desire, and understanding of the seeker.

Consider a telescope. The finest instrument will blur if it's not in focus. During a reading, Edgar Cayce was tuned to the mental body of the seeker. Hence the seeker's conscious, subconscious, and superconscious were a part of it. To assume that this was merely mechanical, a result of suggestion, would be to oversimplify.

Edgar Cayce also used his own conscious mind to stay focused for a reading. He constantly tried to keep optimistic and upbeat. He made a practice of not reading questions prepared for the readings; he did not want to know anything about the person applying for the information; he insisted that each person make a personal request, because he believed it helped set up a mental bridge; he always encouraged seekers to maintain a prayerful, meditative state during the actual period of the reading. Nevertheless, sometimes his own feelings, such as anger or illness, interfered.

Edgar Cayce said that he could withdraw from the physical body just as one withdraws while asleep and at death. He was then free to move through these levels of consciousness.

He could attune to the subconscious level of another living person and from that level describe physical conditions of the body unknown to physical consciousness. He could also attune to higher levels of consciousness—the aspirations, purposes, and development of the soul-mind. He could tune in to thought-patterns and thought-forms. It was from these that he seemed to draw much of his general health information.

But what took place when Edgar Cayce seemed to

communicate with those on other planes of consciousness?

What are the laws that govern this type of communication? Who did Edgar Cayce communicate with, and why?

In a reading on October 9, 1923, at the Phillips Hotel in Dayton, Ohio, Edgar Cayce was asked:

(Q) Is it possible for this body, Edgar Cayce, in this state, to communicate with anyone who has passed into the spirit world?

(A) The spirit of all that have passed from the physical plane remain about the plane until their development carry them onward or are returned for their development here, when they are in the plane of communication or remain within this sphere, any may be communicated with. There are thousands about us here at present. 3744-3

In a reading on January 17, 1925, at the Cambridge Hotel in New York City, Morton Blumenthal asked:

(Q) What is meant by souls within this sphere may be communicated with by the body, Edgar Cayce, in the psychic state?

(A) Each and every soul entity, or earthly entity, passing through the earth's plane, radiates in that plane those conditions that are radiated from the soul or spiritual entity in the individual. This, then, becomes the fact, the real fact, in the material world. When the body, Edgar Cayce, in the psychic or subconscious condition, is able then to reach all the subconscious minds, when directed to such subconscious minds by suggestion, whether in the material world or in the spiritual world, provided

the spiritual entity has not passed entirely into that
condition where the radiation, or the relative forces,
are superseded by other radiations. Then we only
reach those radiations left in earth's plane that are
taken again when entering in earth's plane, whether
entity [is] conscious of same or not. The consciousness of reaching that condition wherein the physical body may take up that truth known, must be
reached by all. Hence the given expression, the
body, Edgar Cayce, in the subconscious condition,
may communicate with those passed into the spiritual plane.

(Q) In reality, then, the body, Edgar Cayce, in the
psychic state, communicates with thoughts, and
not with the spiritual entities themselves.

(A) With the thoughts, and with the radiation as
is given. Then we have as the illustration of this condition in the body, [900]. We have, when this entity
enters the subconscious, through the medium of
laying aside the conscious mind, and the projection
of the spiritual guide, the father [of 900], the
thoughts, the impressions, as would be given by
that entity, entering the subconsciousness of [900].
Not the spiritual entity's taking form, save in the
subconsciousness of [900].

(Q) Then, may the body, [900], his spiritual guide
recede to that point, or position, where the body,
[900], may no longer receive those radiations?

(A) Not until [900] supersedes those radiations by
creations in radiations of his own, for thoughts are
deeds, and all conditions remain, as given.

(Q) Are those radiations like a vibratory force on
our earth's plane, such as light wave?

(A) May be compared to same, but of the spiritual radiation, and not material radiation; that is,

those radiations as come from spirit form may take form in vibratory radiation of color, or light, through the individual's attunement. 900-22

In a reading on March 17, 1927, at Virginia Beach, Edgar Cayce was asked:

(Q) Is it possible for those that have passed into the spirit plane to at all times communicate with those in the earth plane?

(A) Yes and no—for these conditions are as has been described—that the *necessary* way or mode must be prepared; for as this: Ever has that vibration as is attracted and thrown off been active in the world as is exercised through that called the telephone, but without proper connection, without shorts, without any disturbance, may proper communication be made! These have not always been active to the *physical* body. These are not always in proper accord to be used by the physical body. Just the same in that pattern. Those in the astral plane are not always ready. Those in the physical plane are not always ready. What conditions arise (is asked) that we in the physical plane are not ready? The *mind!* What conditions arise that we in the astral plane are not ready? There are those same elements as has been outlined, of that of the development going on, and the willingness of that *individual* to communicate, as given, see? but when set aright, these may—until [they have] passed into that Oneness, or returned again, or gone on beyond such communications.

(Q) What physical thing may an individual do to be able to communicate with those that have passed into the spirit plane?

(A) Lay aside the carnal or sensuous mind and desire that those who would use that mentality, that soul, for its vehicle of expression, do so in the manner chosen by that soul; for some communicate in act, in sight, in movement, in voice, in writing, in drawing, in speaking, and in the various forces as are manifest—for force is *one* force. 5756-4

15

Possession

Once between high school and college I spent a couple of years doing yoga. I didn't have a teacher; I started with one, but decided I was much faster than that. I could do it with a few books by myself. I spent a lot of time and energy on it. My thoughts were in the right spot and so were my dreams. Fine. So I drove myself. One day, curled up in the middle of the floor, in my room at Virginia Beach, suddenly something clicked. And I was out of my body.

I was way away from my body. I knew my body was back of me, sitting there, curled up on the floor, and I had my back to it, and I was way down a dark tunnel—a horribly dark tunnel, oppressively dark. And there was this monster—not very pleasant looking—something like an amoeba, a woozy, goozy glob of jellyfish. But magnified. And It was moving toward my body, with the intent of swallowing it, possessing it, taking it over. As It moved toward my body, It moved toward me at the same time. And I willed to try to stop It and started to back up, and it was this horrible dream of fright, movement, intense pain, and suffering, of that Thing getting closer and closer—me backing up, backing up, backing up. I used every affirmation, everything I knew to keep that Thing away as I backed up. And only by naming the Name was I able to check It at all.

Then, click, I was back in my body again. And I knew what I'd been looking at—all of the vile thoughts, all of the negativity I had poured out perhaps for many lives— right there in front of me. I'd been looking at myself— that which I myself had created.

Until that day I had never been on that level of consciousness, or that plane, and I never want to go back there again. I have had enough of it.

It was a good experience for me, because it started me on a different pattern of searching.

I think we all, now and then, add to those monsters around us. Our fears really are reflections of the thought images we create, and they're right there, inside us, tacked on the wall of that plane of consciousness I visited that day.

Possession is believed by some to be a condition pertaining only to biblical times. The readings refute this and give definite warnings about how to avoid it.

In a reading on March 26, 1936, at Virginia Beach, for a psychologist, thirty-five, this was stated:

Hence there be many phases, many characters of the manifestation of psychic forces in the material

world. There are those influences from without the
veil that seek—seek—that they may find an expression, that they may still be a portion of this evolution in the earth, not considering their present
estate. And these bring turmoil, strife. 1135-2

In a previously quoted reading on May 30, 1938, at Virginia Beach, Edgar Cayce told a housewife, forty, of
Catholic background:

We would *not* from here counsel *anyone* to be
guided by influences from without. For the *king-
dom* is from within! 1602-1

For some cases Edgar Cayce cited unwise use of psychic power in past lives. Below I have collected eleven
cases of possession of varying difficulty, with diagnoses
from the readings.

(1) 1572—Couldn't sleep; bothered by tiny dwarfs
crawling all over her; while asleep, believes she is a
man seeking sexual gratification; has gone to witch-
craft doctors trying to get "dispossessed."
Reading—
Glandular disturbance; incoordination between
cerebrospinal and the sympathetic nervous sys-
tems; pressures in lumbar region, in lower dorsal
and brush-end of the spine, overstimulating glandular forces related to the plexus at the pubic bone
itself. This condition is not possession.
(2) 4787—Hallucinations.
Reading—
Lesions in the pelvic area. Not possession.
(3) 1183—Husband drank heavily.
Reading—

(Q) What causes him to lose control of himself?
(A) Possession . . .
(Q) Regarding my husband, what is meant by "possession"?
(A) Means *possession!*
(Q) Does that mean by other entities, while under the influence of liquor?
(A) By others while under the influence that causes those reactions and makes for the antagonism, and the very *change* of the activities.

. . . if there could be a sufficient period of refraining from the use of alcoholic stimulants and the diathermy electrical treatments used these would drive these conditions out!

But do not use same with the effects of alcohol in the system—it would be detrimental! 1183-3
(4) 3380—Severe headaches; unable to sleep.

Reading—
Result of injury; psychological condition of an unusual nature. Here there is the attempt of possession during periods when the body relaxes.
(5) 3421—Woman described "a creature" which attacked her; as seen by clairvoyants, a huge octopus, which produced violent nerve reactions, jerking of body, and severe pain. She had visited all kinds of doctors and worked with various metaphysical organizations without relief.

Reading—
We find that there has been the opening of the Lyden [Leydig?] gland, so that the kundaline forces move along the spine to the various centers that open with this attitude, or with these activities of the mental and spiritual forces of the body—much in the same manner as might be illustrated in the foetus that forms from conception. These naturally

take form. Here these take form, for they have not in their inception been put to a definite use.

The psychological reaction is much like that as may be illustrated in one gaining much knowledge without making practical application of it. It then forms its own concepts.

Now we combine these two and we have that indicated here as a possession of the body; gnawing, as it were, on all of the seven centers of the body . . . 3421-1

It was advised that packs be used over the area of the ovaries and osteopathic corrections be given in the coccyx area. The second reading indicated improvement. It also contains an interesting reference:

. . . the body allows itself to slip back into that consciousness to be controlled by the formation of that which is as a positive possession—but a creation of the own mental and physical self. 3421-2

(6) 422—Hallucinations; heard voices.

Reading—

Indicated that the individual had been curious about psychic phenomena, had played with them. In another life, this entity had used occult power to control others. This might lead to possession in this life, unless corrected.

(7) 386—Hallucinations; heard voices; nervous speech.

Reading—

Caused by shocks and suppression, from eighth to twelfth year.

Not possession.

(8) 3000—Woman concerned about influence trying to put her to sleep at night.

Reading—

Recommended use of low electrical appliance. The influence could not work through the low electrical forces. When asked the source of this influence, the reading indicated that it resulted from attempts by others to impose themselves upon the entity. The person who received this reading also suffered from a blood deficiency.

(9) 3662—Considered a manic-depressive case; in an institution when reading was given.

Reading—

... unless proper corrections are made, there must eventually be caused a full possession ... there are those pressures existing in the coccyx, and in the lower lumbar and sacral areas, that have prevented and that do prevent the normal closing of the lyden [Leydig] gland ... 3662-1

(10) 5405—Mental collapse; shock treatments; insulin; institution.

Reading—

Dementia praecox. No obsession, no possession.

(11) 5221—Nervousness; supersensitivity.

Reading—

(Q) How did I happen to pick this up?

(A) ... the body in its study opened the centers and allowed self to become sensitive to outside influences.

(Q) What is it exactly that assails me?

(A) Outside influences. Disincarnate entities.

5221-1

Even so few as these eleven readings are startling. They recognize possession as a distinct possibility and suggest ways to eliminate the danger: keep the physical body in good condition—free from glandular disturbance and free of lesions in the lower spine; keep the blood free from deficiencies, such as low hemoglobin, deficient white corpuscles, and abnormal sedimentation rate—all of which can be detected by a physician.

I should also emphasize that similar symptoms are present during possession and during physical disturbances appearing to be possession. Notice the close relationship between the lower spinal areas and the endocrine glands (lyden and gonads) in the lower portion of the body.

Possession can evidently include not only influences from what Theosophists call the "lower astral," but also influences from thought-forms created by individuals themselves in this and other life experiences. A fine line can be drawn here, and one should not jump to conclusions. Symptoms alone cannot be the basis; some of the cases described above show more signs of possession than others.

In a reading on November 25, 1936, at the David Kahn home in Scarsdale, New York, an electrical engineer, forty-two, asked:

(Q) To further my work in possible radio reception of cosmic messages, should I attempt to train myself in automatic handwriting, or use a medium?

(A) As has been indicated, rather than *automatic* writing *or* a medium, turn to the voice within! If this then finds expression in that which may be given to the self in hand, by writing, it is well; but not that the hand be guided by an influence outside of itself. For the universe, God, is within. Thou art His. Thy communion with the cosmic forces of nature, thy communion with thy Creator, is thy birthright! Be satisfied with nothing less than walking with Him! 1297-1

In a Search for God reading on August 7, 1932, at Virginia Beach, one group member asked:

(Q) [2125]: You told me that anyone could do automatic writing. Will you please tell me how I may develop it?

(A) By practice. Sit alone with pencil and paper, and let that guide that may be sought—or may come in—direct. It will come. Anyone may; but is it the better may oft be the question? This may only be the better when surrounding self with those influences that may bring those of the *constructive* forces alone. 262-25

In a reading on June 20, 1934, at Virginia Beach, for an A.R.E. group considering a paper on automatic writing, Cayce said:

As to the activities of what may be termed the channels through which individuals may receive inspirational or automatic writings, the inspirational is the greater of the activities—yet may partake of both the earth-earthly things and the heaven-heavenly things, while the automatic may partake only of that source or force which is impelling, guiding or directing. The inspirational may develop the soul of the individual, while the automatic may rarely reach beyond the force that is guiding or directing.

To some this is satisfactory. So is the satisfying of carnal forces satisfying to some. So are those things for the moment alone gratifying to the extreme. But he that would know the better will find that the *soul* of the entity must be in the attitude of seeking, knocking, and in attune with that which he would

receive. And thus may the soul—whether from this,
that or the other channel of activity through the experiences of the soul in finding expression in any
relationships with those things that may make for
developments to same—find, in seeking through its
relationships with *its* Creator, that which will make
for the greater development. 5752-4

In a reading at my request as manager of the A.R.E.,
on December 16, 1936, at Virginia Beach, Edgar Cayce
said:

For do not consider for a moment . . . that an individual soul-entity passing from an earth plane as
a Catholic, a Methodist, an Episcopalian, is something
else because he is dead! He's only a dead Episcopalian, Catholic or Methodist. And such personalities
and their attempts are the same; only that *ideal!* For
all are under the law of God equal, and how did He
say even as respecting the home? "They are neither
married nor given in marriage in the *heavenly* home
but are *one!*" 254-92

In a previously quoted life reading on January 29,
1944, at Virginia Beach, a jeweler and optometrist, fifty-
eight, was told:

Be sincere with yourself and other outside influences, even disincarnate entities with and through
whom ye may obtain much, will be sincere with
you. 3657-1

People often ask if I've heard from Edgar Cayce since
he died. The answer is, yes. I've had many dreams about
him. About Gertrude, too.

I had one experience that involved my mother, the kind of thing that really shakes you up. If you've had anything that even faintly resembles this, you wonder about it for a long time.

My mother, before her death, had had a life reading from my father. In it he gave her a life seal. This is a plaque that looks like a coat of arms, a set of symbols that he suggested she have painted and put up where she could see it, because it would talk to her unconscious.

You know, like a beautiful scene in a stained-glass church window, or a chalice on the altar, or a cross, or a dove and an olive branch, or all those things we use as symbols.

In that life seal were two red roses—stems crossed. Mother had her life seal painted. The readings said that for her these red roses symbolized her two sons—my brother and me. She liked this life seal, put it up, and kept it near her. So it was when the Second World War came, and I left; and while I was overseas, she died, and my father died.

When I got back, Florence Edmonds, a close friend of my mother's, said, "Hugh Lynn, I've had a very interesting dream about your mother, and she told me in the dream to tell you that when she communicated with you, she would give you two red roses."

Now this is very interesting, because, if you get that kind of identification for someone, it's like a password. If somebody's standing on the outside of a door and that person gives you the right password, you open it up and let that individual in. But if you don't know who's on the other side of the door, you don't open the door until you look through the peephole or ask some questions.

So I had a password for Gertrude Cayce—something she would use to communicate.

Years passed, and I got communications from everybody under the sun. They all thought they'd talked to
Edgar Cayce. They talked to him through automatic writing and Ouija boards. They talked to him through mediums, and they talked to him in dreams. They talked to
him in all kinds of ways, and I got hundreds of them!
From Gertrude Cayce, too! But I hadn't gotten any red
roses, and the information didn't seem accurate or very
helpful.

About twenty-five years after Mom died, a man called
one day from a large eastern city and said, "Mr. Cayce,
my wife has had a lot of trouble, and she wants to talk to
you. But I must explain. She got ahold of a Ouija board
about a year ago, and from the Ouija board she went into
automatic writing, and from automatic writing she began to hear voices. They began to bother her and frighten
her, and so she went to a doctor. He put her in a mental
institution and gave her some shock treatments and
whatnot; she's now home again, and still hearing the
voices, but she's not telling the doctor. She's hearing
these voices, and she thinks you can tell her what they're
saying. Some of them are horrible. She writes this stuff
down. It's like garbage. It's terrible. We're having an awful
time at our house. Will you talk to her?"

I said, "Sure," and we set a time when the husband was
supposed to call back.

So at three o'clock that afternoon, the phone rang, and
he said, "I'll be on the other line, and I'll cut her off when
you want to get off, because these voices don't stop and
she won't get off the line."

So he put her on and she began to tell me what she
was hearing. The husband was right—it was garbage. It
was very much like you'd stand on the corner of a big
city and listen to the conversations of everyone going
by—everyone! Some, you know, were pretty awful. Some

were prophecies of dire destruction, and some were dog-
gerel poetry, simple little sayings, bits and pieces. As if
thousands of people were talking to her.

As I listened, I began to pray for her.

Well, she talked and I prayed for ten or fifteen minutes, and suddenly she said, "Mr. Cayce, your mother
says to give you two red roses." And she hung up.

Three days later, the husband called back and said,
"Mr. Cayce, we want to come to see you. Do you know
that since my wife talked to you, since she told you that
your mother was giving you two red roses, she hasn't
heard a voice. She's healed."

Well, they came to see me, you know, two of the nicest
A.R.E. members you'll ever lay your eyes on.

So what worked here to end this woman's possession?
Prayer, certainly. Also, perhaps, a little help from Mother
on the other side.

16

Angels, Guides, Ideals, and the Christ

Angels

In a reading on June 17, 1933, for about thirty attending the second A.R.E. Congress at Virginia Beach, Edgar Cayce was asked about angels and archangels. He replied:

> With the bringing into creation the manifested forms, there came that which has been, is, and ever will be, the spirit realm and its attributes—designated as angels and archangels. They are the spiritual manifestations in the spirit world of those

attributes that the developing forces accredit to the
One Source, that may be seen in material planes
through the influences that may aid in development of the mental and spiritual forces through an
experience—or in the acquiring of knowledge that
may aid in the intercourse one with another.
5749-3

A life insurance agent, thirty-four, in a business reading in Virginia Beach on February 21, 1934, asked Cayce:

(Q) Are there any individuals or groups that I
should seek to contact . . .
(A) . . . Not as to who; for, as has often been given,
be ye mindful in every association and manner
when ye entertain strangers, for often ye entertain
angels unawares. 520-3

Note that Edgar Cayce pointed this man away from
known individuals and groups to whomever he might
meet—strangers—and angels—thereby broadening his
scope.
A Protestant housewife, twenty-one, in a reading on
June 9, 1934, in Virginia Beach, asked:

(Q) For what vocation am I best fitted?
(A) For the greatest vocation of all—home.
(Q) How can I best prepare myself for it?
(A) Look within and know that self is in accord, in
attune, with that He has given is the better way for
such activities. For His blessings, His actions were
as He gave, "I go to prepare a place, that where I am
ye may be also." Then, in the home, prepare such
that all who may enter—the stranger, the foe, the
friend and the brother—may find it a joyous place,

one wherein they oft desire to be. For, those who have entertained others have oft entertained angels unawares. 578-2

A reference to guardian angels comes from a life reading for a soldier who was left for dead on the battlefield during the First World War. He had a strange experience of being helped.

In the angel stooping on the field, in the walking through the garden with the shadow about same— the entity was being guided, or guarded, or protected, that that as had been promised from the foundations of the world would be to each individual, "If ye will be my people I will be thy God." He that walketh in the light, and purposes in his heart to *do, be,* that which *the* Creative Forces would *have* one be, shall *not* be *left* alone! for though he walk through the valley of the shadow of death, His arm, His hand, will direct thy ways. 909-3

The Glad Helpers Prayer and Healing Group, studying the Book of Revelation at Virginia Beach, on February 17, 1937, asked:

(Q) What is meant by the symbol of the angel with the golden censer and the incense described in Rev. 8:3-5?
(A) As the influence is visualized in the experience of each soul by the name as implied in "angel," or the good that goes out from the individual soul in its relationships to the influences or forces about same, so is it called or given as the angel with the censer of the activities that emanate from each individual. And as has been given in other illustra-

tions, that ye *are*—that of good—rises ever as an incense, sweet before the throne of mercy. Or to take
the back track, as it were, and take the angel with
the censer, with the incense that is before the im-
age of a soul seeking to become one with the Creative Forces or God—that which has been kind,
gentle, patient, merciful, long-suffering in self's experience during a day, rises before the throne of the
mercy seat within self to that of an incense of satis-
faction. Why? Hate, unkindness, harshness, all such
become as base in thine own experience, and as
usual one condemns self by saying, "Why can't I do
this or that?" And, "What is the use?" Well—and the
censer is broken! 281-30

In a reading on January 25, 1936, at Virginia Beach, a
chemist, Christian, working in a perfume and cosmetics
lab, was told:

What bringeth the varied odors into the experience of man?
Did lavender ever make for bodily associations?
Rather has it ever been that upon which the angels
of light and mercy would bear the souls of men to a
place of mercy and peace, in which there might be
experienced more the glory of the Father. 274-10

In a reading on November 21, 1933, in Staten Island,
New York, a woman harpist, twenty, Protestant, who
asked how to attune herself to the Creative Forces
through music, was told:

See, through the intuitive self, the spirit of that
which *impelled* the recorder of the notes or the
music, and there is aroused in self then that which

will make for periods when not of self but rather as of angels in the seraphim choir will be the activity; rather as of the spirit of truth. For, know ye well that the Prince of Peace was a harpist Himself! 275-35

In a previously quoted reading given in New York City on January 22, 1934, for an executive, forty-six, a Spiritualist, Edgar Cayce said:

> For, as has been given, when thou hast shown in thine heart thy willingness to be guided and directed by *His* force, He gives His angels charge concerning thee that they bear thee up and prevent the stumblings that come to the sons of the Creative Forces in and among the sons of men. 423-3

While writing the Search for God lesson, "What Is My Ideal?" with Norfolk Study Group #1, on January 10, 1932, Edith Edmonds, who'd been told she had been Martha, sister of Lazarus at the time of Jesus, asked about a dream:

> (Q) . . . I was in a boat, suspended quite high from the deck, seemingly in a hammock which rocked to and fro over the side of the deck. I realized there was an ocean beneath and if I was thrown out what the result would be. Then the words came, "Not my will but Thine, O Lord, be done." I then saw, as it appeared to me, in the heavens a beautiful white-robed angel. Please interpret.
> (A) As seen, an emblematical vision of self's own awakening to the conditions about self, those associated with self, and the source of help and aid as may come through the combined efforts of those as indicated by the character of the group, and by

the character of the hammock or boat as seen. In a
sea, or maze, are many. As the white light of truth is
made manifest in the hearts and souls of many, will
peace, harmony, contentment, joy of service come
to all. 262-9

Guides

In a reading on January 8, 1934, in Virginia Beach, a
forty-five-year-old mother, club member, society leader,
and Theosophist, asked:

(Q) Has each soul an individual guide?

(A) Each soul has been given, we have given that
each soul *has* an individual guide—but the more
often does such rise or develop by the choosing. As
has been given, "There is set before thee life and
death, good and evil—choose thou." But it is just as
true, "His angels have been given charge concerning thee" . . .

(Q) Who is my highest personal teacher?

(A) That should be sought rather by self than to
be given even from here. For, as ye name the
Name—this to the soul should mean, and does
mean, that which is not to be spoken.

(Q) Are Krishnamurti's teachings the highest?
[Jiddu Krishnamurti, b. 1897 in Adyar, Madras, India (Center of the Theosophical Society)]

(A) Highest that Krishnamurti may give!

(Q) Are they the highest being given today?

(A) Dependent upon who is the judge, and who
and what the ideal—as is set. These are high—*very*
high. 443-3

Krishnamurti broke from the Theosophical Society in
1927-29, because of a Messianic expectancy he felt there.

Publishers of his books in 1953-54 commented: "He was educated in England from childhood. He followed Hindu Gurus, but arrived at new interpretations. He was widely known on three continents as an author and speaker of exceptional clarity and appeal."

A reading in New York City on January 22, 1934, for an executive, forty-six, a Spiritualist, gave this information:

(Q) Please give name and history of highest spirit guide assigned to my wife and me.

(A) These had best be sought in self. Not that these may not be given, for they are present with thee in thy activities; but "What is thy name?" that has been sought by others, and as the answer came then, "What meanest these experiences in thy life?" so may the name come to thee, even as it did to Elkannah [Elkanah—1 Sam. 1:21; husband of Hannah, father of Samuel] as he offered the sacrifice, as he offered meat—for he is thy guide.

(Q) Has he any instructions as for our contact with him?

(A) Seek and ye shall find. Put into application that thou knowest day by day, for it is line upon line, precept upon precept, here a little and there a little that ye gather together those forces that make for the greater material manifestation of those influences in thy daily experience that may bring thee to the consciousness, to the understanding of those forces that would aid thee. 423-3

On September 19, 1931, in Virginia Beach, this dialogue occurred between a railroad agent, twenty-nine, Protestant and Rosicrucian, and the sleeping Edgar Cayce:

(Q) Who is giving this information?

(A) That same that stood in the position for the entity as a guide, and an aide, and that one who may be termed the guardian of this entity's activities— Demetrius . . .

(Q) What is Demetrius at present?

(A) The body's guardian angel. As he stood and reasoned with Paul, again as he stood as the *aide* to Paul *in* the spirit world. *This entity* in attune *with* that *as was* given by *this* entity as the messenger in Egypt—for Demetrius *there, again,* the brother and the aide in the flesh. 311-6

It seems that this man's guardian angel was an entity on another level of consciousness, but had been a brother in a prior incarnation. Ties between them lie in the mental realm and relate to ideas, ideals, and purposes. This reinforces the concept that we are much more closely related to souls in the realm of the mind than we may ordinarily think. Such relationships would exist between entities both in and out of physical bodies. The term *angel,* by the way, in this case is used to describe a protective soul, not strictly a celestial being.

In a previously quoted reading on January 8, 1934, in Virginia Beach, a forty-five-year-old mother, club member, society leader, and Theosophist, asked:

(Q) How high is this source [of] information . . .

(A) From the universal forces, and as emanated through the teacher that gives same—as one that has been given—Halaliel. 443-3

Halaliel will be discussed in the next chapter.

Ideals

In a reading at Virginia Beach on February 8, 1934, an electrical engineer, twenty-three, student and Christian, asked Edgar Cayce:

> (Q) Do you find that I do not know my ideal?
> (A) ... What thou hast done is lovely, but knowest thou *in* what it is lovely? In thine own mind, or in the glory to God? In the development of thine self, or in *exaltation* or in the activities of self? For, not selfish aggrandizement—nay, my son, no selfish purpose enters in; but let not thy right hand know what thy left hand doeth. What meaneth this? That, as step by step, thou wilt follow in the ways as *He* has opened before thee. For, above all, keep thy *balance* in spirit, in truth, in body, in mind, as has been given thee; else thou may lose thy way! But put thyself in that position where He may give His angels charge concerning thee, and never "Let's see what will happen." 440-14

In a reading on December 31, 1943, at Virginia Beach, Edgar Cayce told a woman, fifty-nine, an office worker:

> So live, then, that at the passing of this particular phase of thy experience—in what man calls death— thy abilities may still be creative in the minds, hearts and activities of others, even unto the third and tenth generation when ye may again enter and enjoy those relationships that ye have longed or sought for and apparently have lost in this experience ... 3611-1

In another reading, the woman harpist, twenty, [275], who'd been told she could design life seals, asked for

help with meditation on December 12, 1933, at Virginia
Beach. She was told:

> Rather would we refer the body-mind to that
> which has been given in how to open self, in medi-
> tation, and what physically takes place; as to how
> the body chooses that manner of cleansing, physi-
> cally, mentally, and how the body surrounds itself
> with that consciousness of His angels having been
> given charge concerning thee. 275-36

In a life reading for a housewife, thirty-nine, on November 23, 1943, at Virginia Beach, Edgar Cayce said:

> Do not put anything before the divine purpose
> within self. For all that each soul may know of the
> Creator is that which will answer to the spirit of
> truth as the entity deals with the problems of the
> day. For it is here a little, there a little. God's pur-
> pose is ever growth. For ye grow in grace, in knowl-
> edge, in understanding. And this ye may accomplish
> here and now. Ye have a will of thine own, one at
> times adamant as to what others say or do. And yet
> it is in patience that ye are to learn in this experi-
> ence. Not a passive thing. Patience is not a passive
> thing, it is an active principle in the ideals and pur-
> poses of each soul. 3416-1

In a reading on March 5, 1933, Minnie Barrett of Norfolk Search for God Study Group #1 during the lesson,
"The Lord Thy God Is One," asked:

> (Q) . . . Please tell me to whom was I talking the
> morning of Feb. 3rd and just why am I getting this
> experience.

(A) As given, be not afraid when it is said, "It is I." Rather, then, the experiences that are necessary for making aware within the consciousness of self how the inner self may be controlled by those powers, those influences, that an entity, an individual, entertains. Be not unmindful that ye entertain strangers that come to thee in thine consciousness, that reaches to the inner self and to the cosmic spheres; for angels are often entertained. Then, clothe and feed them only upon the words and the activities of the spirit of truth, and through same may come those experiences that have been long sought; for the time is near at hand. 262-40

The Christ

On August 6, 1933, at Virginia Beach, in a special reading on Jesus, Minnie Barrett asked:

(Q) Is Jesus the Christ on any particular sphere or is He manifesting on the earth plane in another body?

(A) As just given, all power in heaven, in earth, is given to Him who overcame. Hence He is of Himself in space, in the force that impels through faith, through belief, in the individual entity. As a Spirit Entity. Hence not in a body in the earth, but may come at will to him who *wills* to be one with, and acts in love to make same possible.

For, He shall come as ye have seen Him go, in the *body* He occupied in Galilee. The body that He formed, that was crucified on the cross, that rose from the tomb, that walked by the sea, that appeared to Simon, that appeared to Philip, that appeared to "I, even John." 5749-4

Was this the beloved disciple, John? Those present assumed so. It echoed the words of Cayce as he began the reading:

Yes, we have the group as gathered here; and their work, their desires. We will seek that as may be given at this time.

"I, John, would speak with thee concerning the Lord, the Master, as He walked among men. As given, if all that He did and said were written, I suppose the world would not contain all that may be said." 5749-4

Minnie Barrett continued:

(Q) Wherever He is, how may I contact Him so that I may see Him and hear Him speak?
(A) The making of the will of self one with His will makes a whole attunement with Him. He *will*, with the making of self in accord and desiring same, speak with thee. "Be not afraid, it is I." 5749-4

During this reading, and all others in which Edgar Cayce conveyed the thoughts of another entity, his voice remained unchanged, normal, ever the man we knew as Edgar Cayce.

Two weeks later on August 20, 1933, at Virginia Beach, while the Search for God Group, Norfolk #1, was writing the lesson, "Opportunity," Minnie Barrett asked:

(Q) . . . As was given in the reading by John, how may I make my will more in accord with His will, that He *will* speak with me?
(A) As He has given to those to whom He spoke, to those to whom He will speak: "If ye love me, keep

my commandments. If ye love me, feed my sheep. If ye love me, feed my lambs."

So, in the experience of all that seek to know His biddings, do with the might that the opportunity presents to thee in each day's activity.

Be not impatient, but know that He will not tarry—to those who love Him and keep His biddings.

(Q) Where am I falling short?

(A) Who am I, that would speak against any fault in any soul? Seek rather to find the fault from thine own inner self, and He will guide thee aright.

So spake He to those that asked of Him, and so speaks He to those that seek. For, "My Spirit beareth witness with thy spirit" to all that love His coming. 262-51

In a reading on October 21, 1931, Florence Edmonds, who'd been told she'd been a sister of the Prince of Peace when He had been Zend in a previous incarnation, asked:

(Q) Might I receive at this time a message from the Master?

(A) Come, mine daughter, mine sister. In choosing me, as I have chosen you, there comes that beauty of oneness in knowing the way that brings to others peace, joy, happiness, in *doing His* will; for he that seeks to do *His* will may *in* me have that peace, that joy, that understanding, that gives to each in their *respective* spheres their needs, their desires, as their desires are in me. Be faithful then, even as thou wert faithful *then*. 993-3

Here, apparently, Cayce was relaying the thoughts of the Master.

In a special reading on Jesus for the Glad Helpers
Prayer Group on March 12, 1941, at Virginia Beach, while
Germany was wreaking havoc in Europe, Edgar Cayce
said:

> There should be the reminding that—though He
> bowed under the burden of the Cross, though His
> blood was shed, though He entered into the tomb—
> through that power, that ability, that love as mani-
> fested in Himself among His fellow men He broke
> the bonds of death; proclaiming in that act that
> *there is no death* when the individual, the soul, has
> and does put its trust in Him. 5749-13

In a reading for a widow, sixty-four, Protestant, on
June 16, 1940, at Virginia Beach, Edgar Cayce said:

> For there is no death, to those who love the Lord;
> only the entering into God's other chamber . . .
> These are the promises, then, which He so easily
> and so well gave, "If ye love me, ye will keep my
> commandments, and I and the Father will come
> and abide with thee. Lo, I am with you always, even
> unto the ends of the world."
> It is not the end, then, because we pass from one
> room to another, from one consciousness to an-
> other. For, so is it proclaimed in that promise.
> 2282-1

In a reading for a woman, forty-six, Protestant, on December 2, 1936, at the David Kahn home in Scarsdale,
N.Y., Edgar Cayce said:

> For death hath no sting, it hath no power over
> those that know the Resurrection, even as thou hast

seen and as thou hast known, as thou hast heard,
how the Resurrection brought to the consciousness
of man that power that God hath given to man, that
may reconstruct, resuscitate, even every atom of a
physically sick body, that may resurrect even every
atom of a sin-sick soul, may resurrect the soul that
it lives on and on in the glory of a resurrected, a re-
generated Christ in the souls and hearts of men!
1158-5

17

Halaliel

After the Cayce Hospital closed in February 1931, a group of from twelve to eighteen friends gathered around Dad, seeking spiritual guidance. In effect, we said to him: We'd like to be able to do what you do—can you show us how? In effect, he replied: I don't know; let's try it and see what happens. The group, including me, called itself Search for God Study Group, Norfolk #1.

Starting in September 1931, we received 130 readings in the 262 series over the course of eleven years; the last was given in July 1942. These consisted of short discourses suggested by the sleeping Cayce, such as "Cooperation," "Know Thyself," and "What Is My Ideal?" For each lesson he gave us an affirmation to be kept in our attention for fifteen minutes daily. We were encouraged not to accept these spiritual precepts blindly, but to test them in our lives.

In October 1933, while the nation was recovering from the Depression and our Search for God Group was wavering, and Dad was suffering economic shortfalls and ill health, Edgar Cayce began conveying thoughts from an angel who called himself Halaliel. Now Halaliel was, as defined by the readings, "One in and with whose courts Ariel fought when there was the rebellion in heaven." (262-57)

Though Dad maintained his voice, manner, inflection, and tone in readings during this period, as always, Halaliel offered to direct the readings in a clearer, more organized fashion. It was indicated that we, the group, needed to decide whether or not to accept this offer. Personally, I did not believe that this was necessarily the angel, Halaliel. Over a period of several readings and after much discussion, Study Group #1 decided that its purposes and guidance should continue to focus on the Christ Consciousness, that we would not accept Halaliel's offer.

Two members raised questions about the possibility of having both the offered guidance and what all agreed was a higher attunement with the Christ Consciousness.

It was for all a period of questioning, testing, and decision.

As I understand the readings which followed, the group was commended for the choice and stand which had been taken.

On one occasion after a reading with Eileen Garrett, her spirit guide, Uvani, offered to clarify the readings, and a question was asked whether this would be wise or not. Again, the offer was not accepted because of a statement in the reading itself. I think this was a similar kind of diversion brought on by the stress and trial through which the whole group and the nation were passing, and because of Edgar Cayce's poor health at the time. During this period, Dad continued to give almost two readings a day for those seeking his help.

Halaliel first addressed the Search for God group in a reading on October 15, 1933, in Virginia Beach, during the lesson, "Day and Night":

> *Come*, my children! Ye no doubt have gained from the comment this day a new initiate has spoken in or through this channel; Halaliel [?], that was with those in the beginning who warred with those that separated themselves and became as naught. 262-56

At a subsequent gathering on January 7, 1934, in Norfolk, we asked:

> (Q) Who is Halaliel, the one who gave us a message on Oct. 15th?
> (A) One in and with whose courts Ariel fought when there was the rebellion in heaven. Now, where is heaven? Where is Ariel, and who was he? A companion of Lucifer or Satan, and one that made for the disputing of the influences in the experiences of Adam in the Garden. 262-57

In other words, Halaliel was one who fought against evil, in particular Ariel, who was a companion of Lucifer or Satan.

On January 19, 1934, in a reading on prophecy and earth changes at the Hastings' home in New York City, Cayce said:

For ye in your weakness [pause] have known the way, through that as ye have made manifest of the *spirit* of truth and light that has been proclaimed into this earth, that has been committed unto the keeping of Him that made of Himself no estate but who brought into being all that ye see manifest in the earth, and has declared this message unto thee: "Love the Lord thy God with all thine heart," and the second is like unto it, "Love thy neighbor as thyself." Who is thine neighbor? Him that ye may aid in whatsoever way that he, thy neighbor, thy brother, has been troubled. Help him to stand on his own feet. For such may only know the acceptable way. The weakling, the unsteady, must enter into the crucible and become as naught, even as He, that they may know the way. I, Halaliel, have spoken. 3976-15

In a previously quoted reading on February 3, 1934, at the Zentgraf home on Staten Island, Mrs. Eileen Garrett, medium for spirit guide, Uvani, asked:

(Q) What entity is giving this information now?
(A) Being directed, as has been indicated, from the records through Halaliel. 507-1

Another mention occurred again September 9, 1934, in Norfolk, while the Search for God Study Group, Norfolk #1, was focusing on the lesson, "Desire."

To all we would give: Be patient. That part thou hast chosen in such a work is born of truth. Let it come in and be a part of thy daily life. Look in upon the experiences, for, as will be seen, my children, there has been appointed one that may aid thee in thy future lessons, and he will be thy teacher, thy guide, [Halaliel?] one sent through the power of thine own desires. Thine own selves, then, may present his being, meeting, living, dwelling, with thee. Not the Christ, but His messenger, with the Christ from the beginning, and is to other worlds what the Christ is to this earth.

As many of you ask now, "Why should the realm of spirit be mindful of this group, of the work of these gathered here?" The sincerity of thy purpose has merited, has destined, that such can be thy experience. "What, then," ye ask, "is the way, the manner?"

That no one mention *who*, though the name and the activities of any desire may be given thee, but when thou speakest outside thine own group, thou hast cut thyself aloof. Art thou willing to accept such a charge? [Pause, of about a minute's duration.] The answers are slow. Some accepted; some know not. Some ask themselves, "What is this?" "In what manner am I approached?"

Ye would enter the Garden with Him and watch while He, as thy Savior, makes intercession for thee. Wilt thou watch? Ye must answer in thine own heart. 262-71

In other words, Halaliel seemed to be coming through because of our desires. Edgar continued:

Now, ye come to that change that must be wrought in thine experiences, would ye give to this seeking, this waiting world that as thou hast, as a group, been prepared for. What is thy destiny, then? What wilt thou give to thy friend, thy neighbor, thy brother, everywhere? Think not that because *that* thou hast given has not received praise and promise and glory from the life, that it has not been heralded abroad as yet, is thine own completing in this lesson that ye must learn. Who of the whole peoples of that city that His Temple of Jehovah had been sat in, looked upon the King on the cross and thought or felt that there would come the day when His words, even, "My peace I give unto you," would change the whole world, and that *time,* even, would be counted from that death, that birth?

So we give, though in [the year] 2034, thy lessons, if they are given in His name, will still be living in the hearts and the souls, even, of those that before the throne of grace will be calling thee by name.

Think ye well, then, on that which has been given thee and choose ye! 262-71

Two weeks later at another Search for God meeting in Norfolk, while the group was trying to reach a decision about Halaliel's clarification offer, Gertrude asked:

(Q) Please explain, so that we may all understand, just what was meant in the last reading, as to the help to be given on the lessons, what we should do, what our approach should be.

(A) Whether that which has been given as lessons to others is to be lived and exemplified in the lives of the members of the group or not, individually, is a choice in the individual—not as a group. This first, as given, must be determined to the best of *their* ability. They, as individuals, as members of the group seeking to be a channel of blessing to someone else, will—with the help of those sources through which they have received inspiration, help, aid—live their own lives in that way and manner as they have asked others to do. Not of themselves; for, as given of old, no soul can say that Christ is come of God *save* the Holy Spirit convict him of that statement. And should one say such and not live the *life* that would exemplify that, then such an one is condemning self already. 262-72

Again at the next meeting on December 23, 1934, in Norfolk the subject was addressed:

Then, quit yourselves as the children of the Most High—and *know* whereunto thou hast chosen that which would be thy direction in this matter.

Some among you are fearful; some are weak; some are doubting; some are seeking more and more. What will ye do with that thou hast chosen? Be strong in Him, for His promises are sure—and ye may walk with Him if ye will choose to be channels of blessings in His name.

Let thy yeas be yea and thy nays be nay in His name, for thou hast chosen the better part—He has chosen thee as thou hast chosen Him. Go ye, then, into the field that is ripe unto the harvest; for His ways are those that lead to eternal life.

Ready for questions.

(Q) Please explain so that we may all understand just—

(A) [Interrupting] All understand much better than they will acknowledge in themselves! Quit ye thyselves like ye believe that thou hast given to thy brother for the directions.

We are through for the present.

[Gladys Davis's note: Two or three in the group were still not convinced that we were right in rejecting Halaliel's help in preparing the lessons.] 262-74

So Dad was warning us not to speak otherwise than
we were willing to act, not to let precept overreach example, or, in other words, to practice what we preach.
Still on the lesson, "Destiny," on January 6, 1935, in
Norfolk, Gertrude opened the next Search for God reading:

> Mrs. Cayce: You will have before you the Norfolk
> Study Group #1, members of which are present
> here, and their desire as individuals to continue
> work on the lessons in fulfilling the purpose of the
> group as a unit. To each individual heart has been
> left the decision to make a new and earnest effort to
> apply the lessons already given to others. As we
> stumble at times, blinded by selfishness, ignorance,
> doubt and fear, we can only turn to the promises of
> our Christ that He will guide and direct if we will
> seek His face. In the name of Jesus, the Christ, we
> seek the light that will guide us along the path He
> would have us go.
>
> Mr. Cayce: . . . What, then, is thy Destiny? It is
> made in that thou pervertest not that thou *knowest*
> to do in thine heart respecting thy fellow man! For
> ye look to Him who is the author and the finisher of
> faith. He *is* Faith, *and* Truth, *and* Light—*and* in no
> other is there comeliness at all. For He is the rock of
> salvation; the bright, the morning star; the rose of
> Sharon; the *wonderful* counselor. In Him *is* thy Des-
> tiny. Turn ye not away from Him. [Gladys Davis's
> note: Again warning not to accept Halaliel or any
> other.] 262-75

At the next Search for God meeting on January 18,
1935, at his home in Virginia Beach Cayce said:

As has been seen from here, what has been given
as to the influences or forces that should be com-
bined through periods of activity—or a certain element for a combination of the mental influences
and forces—is not irrelevant to the better influences for this particular individual or body at this
time. But the attitudes, desires not only of those surrounding or seeking information but of the one
who is receptive—or to act in the capacity of being
receptive for such things—these are well in the
present.

[Gladys Davis's note: (This) seems to be referring
to Edgar Cayce's physical and mental condition,
also to those closely surrounding him during the
readings—particularly to Gertrude Cayce in this instance. Could this also be referring to 262-71 which
indicated that Halaliel was being sent to the group
through their own desires? All the rest of the readings seemed to be counseling the group *against* accepting any other sign or guide along the way
except Jesus, the Christ. Now (this reading) is seeming to say that the obstruction in the mind of Edgar
Cayce and those around him has been removed,
and that all is well. In my mind the above seems to
be somewhat of an apology for the allowing of such
interferences to enter from time to time.] 262-76

Still on the lesson "Destiny," in Norfolk on January 20,
1935, the group was told:

The signs, the omens then, are to be used as stepping-stones for an *understanding;* not to be con-
fused with nor given—through that gift in thee of
constructive forces from the Father-God Himself—

other power than they contain within themselves. For each soul that meets and encounters and accredits receives the same in return. How gave He on this? "He that receiveth a prophet [Halaliel?] in the name of a prophet hath a prophet's reward." This does not indicate that the prophet received is of God, an angel of heaven or of hell; but in the name, in the manner, in the way as received so cometh the reward. *That* is destined! Why? In the seed of thought, whether of body, mind or soul, *is* the seed thereof; and it bears fruit which is of its own kind and nature. Said He, "Ye do not gather grapes from thistles; neither may ye expect to do evil looking for good." For the destiny is in that which has set the world, yea, the earth and all that is therein, in motion. And ye in thy blindness, thy foolishness, thy *desire* for self, look for some *easy* way; when all the ease, all the hope, all the life there is *is* in Him! Then, *His* way is the easy way. What is His way? "He that would force thee to go one mile, go with him twain; he that would sue thee and take away thy coat, give him thy cloak also." Did He say whether justly or unjustly? Who did He say is the judge? "Judge not that ye be not judged." For, "As ye do it unto the least in the earth, ye do it unto me." [Warning regarding accepting Halaliel's offer given in 262-71.] 262-77

The next mention of Halaliel was during a work reading at a temporary office in Washington, D.C., on February 14, 1935, after a lecture there at the Willard Hotel. Edgar Cayce was asked:

(Q) For the better and more rational presentation of the work of Edgar Cayce to the world, will you, if you consider same in order, kindly inform us of

Thine Identity and the source or sources from
which you bring us the information given in answer
to our questions in the readings other than the
Physical? Is it from the Astral—

(A) [Interrupting] From the universal forces that
are acceptable and accessible to those that in ear-
nestness *open* their minds, their souls, to the wonderful words of truth and light.

(Q) To what extent are the Masters of the Great
White Brotherhood directing the activities of Edgar
Cayce? Who are the Masters directly in charge?

(A) *Messengers* from the higher forces that may
manifest from the Throne of grace itself.

(Q) Who are the Masters directly in charge? Is
Saint Germain [Comte de (c. 1710 c. 1780)?]—

(A) [Interrupting] Those that are directed by the
Lord of lords, the King of kings, Him that came that
ye might be one with the Father.

(Q) Is Saint Germain among them? Who is Halaliel?

(A) These are all but messengers of the Most
High. Halaliel is the one who from the beginning
has been a leader of the heavenly host, who has de-
fied Ariel, who has made the ways that have been
heavy—but as the means for the *understanding*.
[Isaiah 29th chapter?]

(Q) Is Saint Germain among them? [Gladys Davis's
note: I understand the Ballard I AM movement was
based on Saint Germain.]

(A) When needed.

(Q) Please give us Thine Identity?

(A) He that seeks that has not gained control
seeks damnation to his own soul! Control thine inner self that *ye* may *know* the true life and light! for
he that would name the Name must have become
perfect in himself!

(Q) If Mr. Cayce is a member and a messenger of
the Great White Brotherhood, how do the Masters
wish him to proceed and should not his activities
henceforth be presented as Their Work?

(A) As the work of the *Master* of masters, that may
be presented when in those lines, those accords
necessary through the White Brotherhood. This—
this—*this,* my friends, even but *limits;* while in Him
is the Whole. Would thou make of thyself, of thyselves,
a limited means of activity? 254-83

18

Michael

A few months before the opening of the Cayce Hospital, while the spirits of the new Association of National Investigators (later renamed the Association for Research and Enlightenment) were running high, at the close of a reading conducted by Morton H. Blumenthal on July 15, 1928, at Virginia Beach, still speaking in his own voice, but louder, Edgar Cayce startled us with an exclamation from Michael, who identified himself as Lord of the Way:

> *Hark!* There comes the voice of one who would speak to those gathered here: [Pause]

*I am Michael, Lord of the Way! Bend thy head, oh
ye children of men! Give heed unto the way as is set
before you in that Sermon on the Mount, in that on
yon hill this enlightenment may come among men;
for even as the voice of the One who stood beside the
sea and called all men unto the way, that those that
would harken might know there was again a staff in
David, and the rod of Jesse has not failed: for in Zion
thy names are written, and in service will come
truth!* 254-42

This utterance in 1928 preceded those of Halaliel by
about five years and would be followed by about a dozen
such utterances until Dad died in 1945, an average of less
than one a year. Half of those occurred during Search for
God Study Group readings, some of which are quoted
below.

At this time much was happening in the Cayce house-
hold—our family relocating, the hospital opening November 11, 1928, then closing February 28, 1931. We
didn't get around to asking directly about Michael until
much later. Cayce identified him in reading 262-28 as "an
archangel that stands before the throne of the Father ...
the lord or the guard of the change that comes in every
soul that seeks the way ... "

The next Michael message occurred in a reading conducted by Edwin Blumenthal, Morton's brother, at
Cayce's office in Virginia Beach on January 13, 1929:

Hark! There would come Him the Lord of the Way
[Michael, the archangel], and he would speak with
thee:

"Bow thine head, for unto *thee* is committed *now*
the keeping of that way in the earth that [man] may
know that the rod has not departed from Judah,

neither has the lion been allayed that rose up in Midian, and unto Him that thou would counsel in teaching my people the ways. Lord of Hosts, be thou near as this, thy servant, bows and calls on those forces as were manifest in the flesh in the way as goeth down by Bethsaida, and as were gathered in the house of Joseph—as in Capernaum many came and kneeled and called thy servant blessed. *He* now is given that charge of he that goes as the light to his people." 900-422

In an April 12, 1931, reading in Virginia Beach, just after the hospital closed, wondering about how next to proceed, we were told by the sleeping Cayce:

In considering an idea and an ideal, *ideas* are worthy of man's consideration—but ideals are something *more;* they must be that as may be sought for, *lived* each day, each hour of each day, would they become not a Frankenstein to those that foster same; for the *spirit* is willing in each, and there is that ability in each to carry forward much as is here set forth, but unless each has so consecrated their lives, their activities, their intents, their purposes *to* the ideal, they will but destroy that which would make for a building of the purposes *in* the lives of others . . .

(Q) Any other advice and guidance for these three?

(A) Thou hast had set before thee that thou art able, wilt thou but *sacrifice* self, wilt thou *crucify* the flesh that the *light* may shine forth.

Hark! Ye children of men bow thine head, for Michael the Lord of the Way would show *thee* thine way—Who is able to stand in the day of the Lord?

He that has purified his heart in the ways that make
for the sons of men to know the Lord of Hosts *would*
approach to thine own throne; for *who* is this Lord?
He that is *holy* is His name! Amen. 3976-7

In a previously quoted reading on August 14, 1931, at
the Hotel Victoria in New York City Vincent Lopez asked:

(Q) Can you contact Azul [Azool? Azrael? Azazel?]
for me?
(A) Demetrius—Michael; Azul—no.
(Q) You cannot?
(A) Cannot.
(Q) Why?
(A) There are barriers between this body and
Azul, as produced by that between Demetrius and
between Michael.
(Q) Can you contact Azul for anyone else?
(A) Not under these conditions; for I, Michael,
speak as the Lord of the Way. Bow thine heads, O ye
peoples, that would seek to know the mysteries of
that life as makes for those *faltering* steps in men's
lives when not applied in the manner as has been
laid down. O ye stiff-necked and adulterous genera-
tion! Who *will* approach the Throne that ye may
know that there is *none* that surpasses the Son of
Man in His approach to *human* experience in the
material world! 2897-4

A reading at Edgar Cayce's home in Virginia Beach on
September 4, 1932, while Search for God Study Group #1
was writing the lesson, "The Open Door," Cayce again
relayed the words of Michael:

Be still, my children! Bow thine heads, that the

*Lord of the Way may make known unto you that
have been chosen for a service in this period when
there is the need of that spirit being made manifest
in the earth, that the way may be known to those that
seek the light! For the glory of the Father will be made
manifest through you that are faithful unto the calling wherein thou hast been called! Ye that have
named the name make known in thy daily walks of
life, in the little acts of the lessons that have been
builded in thine own experience, through those associations of self in meditation and prayer, that His
way may be known among men: for He calls on all—
whosoever will may come—and He stands at the
door of thine own conscience, that ye may be aware
that the scepter has not departed from Israel, nor
have His ways been in vain: for today, will ye harken,
the way is open—I, Michael, call on thee!* 262-27

A member of Search for God Study Group, Norfolk #1,
Ruth LeNoir, thirty-six, Protestant, during a reading at
Virginia Beach on September 14, 1932, asked Edgar
Cayce:

(Q) Was it a true message from Michael that I received Monday morning?
(A) A contact.
(Q) Did I remember the message correctly, and
what was meant by it?
(A) A warning of those conditions, that there be
not a departing from the way in which self has
brought self to an understanding, in its present
concept of true mental and spiritual relationships;
for, as has been given, Michael is the lord of the
Way—and in the *ways* of understanding, of concep-

tion, of bringing about those things that make for the changes in the attitudes in physical, mental or material relationships, is the *guide* through such spiritual relations; for the spiritual is the life, the light, the mental is the builder, the material and physical are the results of those activities as applied in the material, carnal or physical plane. 585-1

Apparently, the archangel was becoming active in the minds of those near Cayce who were sincerely trying to follow the counsel of the readings.

At the next Search for God meeting on September 18, 1932, while the group was writing "The Open Door," Cayce was asked:

(Q) What is the relationship between Michael the lord of the way, and Christ the way?

(A) Michael is an archangel that stands before the throne of the Father. The Christ is the Son, the way *to* the Father, and one that came into the earth as man, the Son of man, that man might have the access to the Father; hence the way. Michael is the lord or the guard of the change that comes in every soul that seeks the way, even as in those periods when His manifestations came in the earth.

Bow thine heads, O ye sons of men, would ye know the way: for I, Michael, the Lord of the Way, would warn thee that thou standest not in the way of thy brother nor sittest in the seats of the scornful, [Ps. 1:1] but rather make known that love, that glory, that power in His name, that none be afraid; for I, Michael, have spoken!

[Gladys Davis's note: The above reading was so powerfully given that many of us were moved to tears; all were touched deeply.] 262-28

The next Search for God meeting on October 2, 1932, in Virginia Beach, while the group was writing "The Open Door," included this question:

(Q) Is there any message for the group as a whole at this time?

(A) Be patient, long-suffering, bearing one another's burdens. Be joyous in the Lord. Be not tempestuous in manner, thought, act or deed; rather *serving* in humbleness of spirit. Enjoy the labors. Enjoy those things that make for the unison of thought in Him, knowing ye have been called, and that "By *His* power I, as a member of such a group, called to give myself first, called that self may become a channel, called that I as an individual may cooperate with my brother *everywhere* in making known the joyous words of the Lord"; for the Lord is in His holy temple, let all the earth keep silent. Who *is* this Lord? Where is His temple? Know ye not that your bodies are the living temple, holy and acceptable unto Him, would ye walk in His ways?

Hark! O ye children of men! Bow thine heads, ye sons of men: for the glory of the Lord is thine, will ye be faithful to the trust that is put in each of you! Know in whom ye have believed! Know that He is Lord of all, and His word faileth not to them that are faithful day by day: for I, Michael, would protect those that seek to know His face!

We are through.

[Gladys Davis's note: Tears, silence, and beautiful attunement followed above reading. Edgar Cayce on waking had a vision during the reading, had to leave the room a while; said he saw each of us as we should be and as we are.] 262-29

Several meetings later, during the lesson, "In His Presence," on December 4, 1932, at Virginia Beach the group asked:

(Q) Is there a message for the group at this time as a whole?
(A) *Bow thine heads, O ye men that would seek His presence!* Be *strong* in His might! Falter not at thine own weak self! Know that thy Redeemer liveth and may *this day make known in thine own heart His presence abiding with thee!* Root from thine body, thine consciousness, aught that would hinder His entering in; for *He* would sup with thee! Wilt thou, then, *O Man*, make known thine own decisions? Will ye be one with Him? The way which I guard leads to that of glory in the might of the Lord. I, Michael, would guide thee. Do not disobey. Do not falter. Thou knowest the way. 262-33

In a reading for the second A.R.E. Congress in Virginia Beach on June 17, 1933, Edgar Cayce was asked:

(Q) Are angels and archangels synonymous with that which we call the laws of the universe? If so, explain and give an example.
(A) They are as the laws of the universe; as is Michael the lord of the Way, *not* the Way, but the lord of the Way, hence disputed with the influence of evil as to the way of the spirit of the teacher or director in his entrance through the outer door. [See Jude 1:9 regarding Michael the archangel "when contending with the devil about the body of Moses" when Moses died.] 5749-3

A reading on November 25, 1940, was given at the

David E. Kahn residence in Scarsdale, N.Y., for a mining engineer, sixty, who was questioning Cayce about where to drill for oil in Texas:

(Q) Can information be given at this time regarding the seeming inaccuracies in previous information regarding the production in the present hole? Please explain as fully as possible.

(A) As has been indicated, there is production here, even in the hole drilled; and there needs be only the waiting for those developments to prove same.

Come! Harken ye children of men! Bow thine heads, ye sons of men! For I, Michael, would speak with thee concerning those things ye question here! Have ye not seen and heard—upon the course that is pursued in the search through this man for knowledge—in such ye deviate at that development of materiality in man's search for God? 1561-19

Undaunted, the mining engineer requested and received two more readings about drilling for oil in Texas, which, to judge by the correspondence, were apparently helpful. Cayce's last reading for this man was given in May 1943 for flu.

Why did Cayce give this and subsequent readings? Because the readings had told him, and he believed that "The Lord is no respecter of persons." He tried to help everyone who came his way, whoever they were, whatever their problem, in whatever manner he could. The readings had affirmed, and he firmly believed, that all of us are "children of the Most High."

On February 24, 1940, Mrs. [1602] wrote to Cayce: "There is one little lady I hope to arrange a reading for. She is the child prophetess, who has been giving verbally the most amazing prophecies since she was six months old—when she began to talk."

In another letter, March 17, she wrote: "The child is really lovely. Natural, sweet, happy, and good, and just radiating light and love. You simply must meet her! And, I think, her mother is equally as lovely . . . "

The readings for this girl, four-and-a-half, contain startling information and an outburst from Michael. In the first reading on March 30, 1940, at Virginia Beach, after warning the mother about the sensitivity of this child and her own purposes as related to her care and upbringing, Cayce said:

> Before this (in its sojourns) we find the entity was among those who were given a special service in the early activities of the Church, in the bringing of spiritual concepts into the minds of individuals through music.
>
> Then the entity was Saint Cecilia—or as Celia the entity was first known—and then known for its abilities in the teaching and ministering to those in the various stages of man's expression and development there—in the Roman activity and experience of the early Church; for the entity brought hope, patience, understanding. 2156-1

Encyclopedias identify St. Cecilia as a Christian martyr and patron saint of music. Cayce continued:

> Then again, before that, we find the entity was in that period from which the greater hope may be expressed; as Elizabeth, the mother of him of whom the Master said, "Among them that are born of woman there hath not risen a greater than John the Baptist."
>
> So, as the entity was a chosen vessel, a chosen

channel for that one who *proclaimed* the day of the Lord to be at hand, the entity now—manifested in that body known as or called [2156]—may indeed be kept as a channel, by those about the entity, that it, too, may arouse and bring the consciousness in the minds of many that the day of the Lord is indeed at hand. 2156-1

The mother of John the Baptist!
In the second reading given in Bronxville, N.Y., on April 16, 1940, Cayce said:

Heed those warnings indicated, to not bring into the experience of the entity—by those who guide or guard the developing years—any who may approach with unbelief.

Rather know, as indicated, those who approach this entity without the consideration of who she is and what she may mean to the world at this time bring on their *own* selves destructive influences; even as those who had the opportunity of having God in their presence and yet believed not . . .

Then—to those who would harken:

Give ye—each one—thanks and praise to thy Maker, through the Christ, the Lord, that ye have been counted worthy to come into the presence of one so endeared to the heart of God, as to have given into thy keeping such a messenger, such a way of manifesting His love in the earth!

Harken to those voices that will again and again proclaim through the entity the *ideals* of the Lord.

Curtail oft those inclinations to seek information concerning those things that would bring or create strife in any section, in any land. 2156-2

Then came this question from the mother:

(Q) Anything else that may be given at this time?
(A) Anything else?!! *Worlds!* Worlds might be filled
with that as might be given!
But let each of you here so live the Christ Consciousness, as manifested in the Master, that you
may be counted worthy to be even as those who
would gather the crumbs of wisdom that will be
manifested through this entity!
*Hark! Ye friends! I, Michael, Lord of the Way, would
give thee warning!*
*Bow thine heads, ye vile ones of the earth! Know
what has been entrusted to thee!*
*Live the life, lest ye be counted accursed for being
unworthy of the trust given thee!* 2156-2

Miss [1387] wrote on October 18, 1940: "We had the
little [2156] there with her mother and father. The
mother talked and showed us the book with all the newspaper clippings and notarized statements, etc., and the
little girl was supposed to give us a message but as those
things always happen she did not . . . She is an elfin little
thing and as you watch her you can see that she is in
touch with something that is beyond the normal ken."
Edgar Cayce responded on October 24, 1940: "The
little [2156] is a darling child—do so hope they will take
the warnings correctly—suppose everyone has his ideas
about such things—but the readings have been right so
many, many times."
The mother wrote to him on November 13. Cayce responded on November 15. The mother wrote again on
December 10: "I am not well physically. Nor have I been
for some time. But I have really had not the time nor the
inclination to dwell on my self. It is only that others are

concerned. However, this I do know, were I to be taken, Mr. [husband] who has done everything under the sun to combat [2156]'s work would see to it that nothing would ever reach the public's ear again. So, you see I have had much to contend with—in my own home ties, much—which I really could not discuss with strangers . . .

"Just now, I have a message to be delivered in-person to the Duke and Duchess of Windsor at Nassau. When and if, [2156] and I will take it to them. I am addressing them to see if they will receive [2156]. The prophecy is one which will change the history of the British Empire."

On July 10, 1941: "Gladys Davis's note: We later learned that [2156]'s parents had separated and that the child was living with her father."

Twenty-two years later, in September 1963, "We heard that [2156] had married, and that her early unhappy life as a 'psychic' had been abandoned when she was separated from her mother."

On October 24, 1964, the mother's second husband wrote of [2156]'s mother's death [the first husband having died earlier] and stated that [2156] and her husband were in the wholesale distributing business in Pennsylvania.

On October 27, 1964, Gladys Davis wrote directly to [2156] asking for details about her life. There was no reply.

Quoting the Bible, the sleeping Cayce often repeated, "Those who have eyes to see, let them see; those who have ears to hear, let them hear." In this case, his warnings seem to have fallen on unhearing ears.

Was Edgar Cayce correct in 1940 when he said that this girl had been St. Cecilia, patron saint of music, and Elizabeth, the mother of John the Baptist? We may never know. The girl herself, now a grown woman, may know.

Either way, does it mean Cayce was wrong about past lives in general? I will discuss that possibility next.

19

Reincarnation

Let's return to Dad's dream of the planes of consciousness. He saw himself as a dot, following the shaft of light through various planes of consciousness to a place where there was sound and color, then to a Hall of Records.

In his attuned state Edgar Cayce was apparently able to reach other rooms of his own and other people's minds. This ability brought about the so-called life readings.

Now Edgar Cayce was not a sophisticated or educated man. He read his newspaper, his Bible, and letters. The few books in our library were gift copies of novels and poetry that Dad had given Mother from his early days as a bookstore clerk. He knew nothing of Buddhism, Hinduism, Rosicrucian literature, or other world religions. When, in 1923, he responded to questions about past lives, the concept went dead against his conscious worldview. It was the same with me. When, at age sixteen, I was introduced to the Cayce readings on past lives, the concept went dead against my worldview, too.

In December 1923, Dad had given up his photo business and was devoting full time to giving readings in Dayton, Ohio. Letters and notes had hinted at financial difficulties, but I was unprepared for the reality.

During my junior year of high school in Selma, Alabama, I joined my family for Christmas. When I got off the train, Dad looked gaunt and worn. It was snowing. He had no overcoat. When I hugged him, I heard the crackling of the newspapers he'd stuffed under his jacket to provide warmth. My spirits fell.

We took a trolley to an apartment upstairs in a small private home in a rundown section of town—the cheapest they could find. Dad kept an office in the old Phillips Hotel where he gave readings. He was afraid to move out because rent was overdue. My train fare, I learned, had been paid with a gold piece my mother had saved for years.

Our dinner was a scrawny chicken, tasty because Mom cooked it, but not much for five people—Dad, Mom, Gladys, my brother, and me. They all seemed happy to have me home, yet I felt a tension, and they seemed to be avoiding my questions. Still, I sensed an excitement. We had hardly finished eating when they began discussing this new kind of reading Dad had been giving and handed me four typewritten pages—my life reading.

I began to read while half listening to this wild conversation about past lives and odd historical characters, presumably us. I began to think, "Are Dad's critics right? Is he really crazy?"

My reading identified several other lives I'd suppos-edly had, most recently as a monk in medieval England. Also a warrior in the Crusades. I had never heard the word *reincarnation.*

"Do you believe this?" I asked Dad.

"I don't know. I'm having to think about it. What do you think?"

"I can't believe it. It's ridiculous," I snorted.

Never in all his ten years of Sunday school classes had I heard him mention past lives from which talents and faults could carry over to the present.

As I continued to read, I got mad. And the more I read, the madder I got. I felt stripped, exposed, opened up like a Christmas package. These pages contained too much about my real feelings and fears, feelings I hadn't con-fided to anybody! My father had betrayed me! I thought he had no right to have said these things in front of Mom and Gladys, let alone put them in print where strangers could pry! I fought back tears and retreated inside my-self; and from that day forward, for the next five years, I ignored the whole idea of reincarnation.

But gradually it dawned on me that this attitude was wrong. Little by little I began to look into the subject se-riously. As I grew older, I was able to articulate my objec-tions:

1. Why don't we remember past lives?

2. Why are there so many kings and queens, so few scullery maids and woodcutters?

3. The airy promise of future lives encourages sin, I thought, because it lets people think they have other chances.

4. It is too fantastic, impossible to prove.

Over the years, trying to apply some objective stan-dards to my skepticism, I've gradually changed my mind about past lives and found what I think are some valid responses to my initial objections:

1. Why don't we remember past lives? I think we do, but not usually on a conscious level. We remember in the shape of our bodies and faces, in our talents and ineptitudes, our likes and dislikes, our loves and fears, our strengths and weaknesses. Sometimes, if we keep our eyes open to possibilities, we can spot solid hints, even glimpses. I'll mention some of my own.

2. Too many kings and queens? Highlights of certain lives would naturally be picked up by someone trying to be helpful, as Dad was. But he also zeroed in on faults and weaknesses.

3. Does the concept encourage sin? On the contrary, a serious study of reincarnation and karmic law will act as a deterrent. "God is not mocked: for whatsoever a man soweth, that shall he also reap." That quote from Galatians 6:7, or abbreviated versions of it, was reiterated by Edgar Cayce in hundreds of readings. If people could accept the idea that current thoughts and actions will cause them to be reborn with friends, families, societies that will either help or hinder them, according to how they treat them in this life, they might find very personal reasons to do good to their fellow humans. Could anything be more fair?

4. Reincarnation may have been impossible to prove in 1923, and probably still is. But I've discovered that my own biggest objection to it had nothing to do with scientific proof. I knew that, if I accepted it, I'd also have to accept responsibility for all my thoughts, attitudes, and actions. If I accepted it, I knew that I could no longer blame anyone else for my thoughts, attitudes, actions. Admitting that my own day-to-day choices widened or closed the gap between me and God was the toughest pill for me to swallow.

Actually, when you think about it in light of what we've already established—that you *are* a soul, you have a body—reincarnation does not seem so fantastic. It is merely the passage of the soul back through God's Other Door into the material realm again.

I've since lived through some startling incidents which to me amounted to personal proof of reincarnation. This concept, incidentally, has been around for centuries. Edgar Cayce did not invent it; he just affirmed it.

Of course, these incidents, which to me were absolutely real, to you will be just stories. They wouldn't hold up in court. They wouldn't be considered proof of anything, just evidence. I don't expect you to change your mind by what I'm about to say. What I hope is that I'll be able to crack a window in your mind, keep you open to the possibility.

In 1926, when I was nineteen, I met a beautiful girl at Norfolk Business College. She played the violin in the Norfolk Symphony. She had light brown hair and ivory skin—one of the most beautiful and talented women I've ever known. To me she was a goddess on a pedestal. I fell in love. We became engaged.

I brought her home to meet my family, and Dad gave her a life reading. It said she'd been my lover in ancient Egypt, but had been stolen away by my best friend in Selma, Alabama, who, according to his own life reading, had been my brother in that life. Neither my fiancée nor my best friend had met. Since I thought all this past-life business was hokum anyway, I decided, as a test, to introduce them to see what would happen.

What happened was that my best friend stole her away again—not only stole her away, but borrowed the family car, took her out alone after he left our house, deceived me while doing it, and ran off with her to New York City.

I had loved that guy like a brother, but after that I wouldn't have trusted him as far as I could throw him by the hind leg. Also, I decided that maybe there was something to past lives after all.

Twenty years later I began to suffer regular choking spells and several times had to be taken to the hospital. Afterward, I dreamed I was choking my former fiancée because she'd been unfaithful and was having someone else's child. This was another life in England, when I was a Norwegian invader. I prayed for forgiveness, for her and for myself. The next morning it was as if a great weight had been lifted.

Though I hadn't heard from her in twenty years, she called a few days later and apologized for the way she'd treated me. I assured her she'd been forgiven.

During the Second World War, I was sitting on a cot at Fort George G. Meade, a big army camp between Washington and Baltimore. I was taking apart a carbine, had it apart on the bed, but was not a bit sure it was ever going back together again. Very simple mechanism, really, but I was not familiar with it.

Since I am a Pisces, my cot was right next to the shower, as usual. This was in the afternoon, and the barracks were practically deserted. Some people were milling around, a couple of boys at the far end of it—big, long barracks with cots on each side.

I began to hear a clop, clop, clop coming down the barracks floor—the wooden clogs of somebody on the way to the shower. As the noise got right opposite me, I looked up, and here was a young man (he turned out to be eighteen; I was thirty-something). He had on only his smile, a towel, a bar of soap, and those wooden clogs. What possessed me I do not know, but as he was opposite me I said, "I haven't seen you since we were caught stealing those camels in the Gobi Desert."

He did a double take, stared at me as if I'd lost my marbles, and marched into the shower. I sat there transfixed because of this scene that had conjured itself in my mind as I said that—three boys, teenagers, around a little fire in the desert, with white racing camels nearby. In the distance I could see people approaching on camels, and I knew these were our families. We were teenagers—and, figuratively, we had taken the family car without permission—and had been racing these camels on the desert. I knew without question that we were about to get one of the worst beatings of all my incarnations. It was a strange terror—a fear of being whipped, of being whipped with canes, badly. And there was no question about whether we deserved it or not. I felt this strange terror!

Now I did not talk to that young man again for a year. He was in another platoon. I was pulled out to do some writing and didn't even get to finish Basic, really. I joined another company, didn't get back to my original platoon again for quite a while, and then went to England.

I was in a Special Services Unit. Our job was to provide recreation—movies, books, live entertainment—for front-line troops. We had all the latest films and portable generators so that we could show them in the field. We had a library of about a hundred movies; they'd drop the latest films to us by parachute. We had music, books, complete shows, singers, magicians, all kinds of entertainment. We serviced the troops in England for a year, then were attached to General Patton's Tank Corps.

That young man came to me in England, gave me a beat-up copy of *There Is a River* that was going around the company, and said, "I'd like to talk to you about this sometime." His name was Sam Benesch. But we didn't cross paths again for months. It was sixteen days after D-day, and we were about to land on the Normandy coast—with several trucks, and pianos, and a complete band—the weirdest stuff to invade Europe with that you ever saw.

Sam turned out to be one of our company's three best hypnotic subjects. An amazing person. The other character in that camel-theft scene was Bill Epstein. I've since found him, too.

Sam and I got better acquainted while waiting for the invasion. One night a bunch of us began fooling around with hypnosis, and Sam volunteered. He was one of three we hypnotized who went back in time and talked in foreign languages. Sam met his grandfather while he was under hypnosis, though his grandfather had died before Sam was born. While he was under, he began talking to his grandfather. He wanted to go with his grandfather, and we had an awful time getting him out of it. His grandfather had taken him on all these trips to India and Egypt. All this took place in front of fifty GIs in a crowded room. And we couldn't wake him up. He'd been talking with his grandfather, whom nobody else could see, of course. I had to slap him and do all kinds of things to get him out of it. He left the room immediately and was upset for days.

I was walking guard that night between 2 and 4 a.m., and Sam came out and walked with me. We talked. As a result of the hypnosis, he remembered all these trips to Egypt and India, strange priestly initiation ceremonies. Being somewhat familiar with Tibetan and Egyptian mysticism, I recognized some of what he told me. He had the widest knowledge. After the incident, I wrote to his mother about it. She remembered that, as a little boy, he had talked about his grandfather coming to him in his sleep and taking him on trips. It frightened them. They'd taken him to a psychiatrist who'd hypnotized him and wiped it all out. We had opened the door again on this whole experience. He'd never known his grandfather except in these dreams. Sam and I hardly left one another's company after that, and we've remained lifelong friends. In 1980 he was an executive for a large corporation.

Years later, the day Germany surrendered, our company was stationed in a little Austrian village in the Bavarian Alps near Berchtesgaden. We'd liberated some fine Austrian beer, and I was consuming a canteen cup of it while seated in the front yard of a neat little cottage. The road through the village was crowded with remnants of the Austrian army—exhausted, bedraggled, scrawny. Prisoners from a nearby work camp, looking lost, tramped along the edge of the road—Poles, Russians, Czechs. American trucks raced back and forth picking up airplane engines cached along the road. British trucks carried a joyous cargo of liberated airmen who'd been shot down in some of the first Romanian oil raids, had been imprisoned for years, and now free, were singing, laughing, shouting, drinking as they headed for flights back to England. Excitement, relief, joy, confusion, and fear melded into an almost tangible wave.

As I sat there soaking in the beer and confusion, something clicked in my head, and I saw before me a marching horde of Crusaders—men in armor on horses, men in leather, carrying spears, servants riding and walking, some with armlets and hooded falcons, dwarfs doing handsprings around the column. I was transported back to the time of the Crusades.

But, as suddenly as they appeared, these images disappeared; a curtain which had parted briefly, closed gently. Yet it left me with a strange geographical awareness. I knew where an old building had stood, where there'd been a stone bridge over a small stream.

Then came a peculiar sense of "It's over," of a cycle having ended. Long ago I had left home and family to fight a war; in this life I'd come back to the very spot from which the departure had been made. I thought of my wife and child back home, of my father and mother who'd died a few months before. I wondered about the patterns of karma, if this were some sort of completion.

All my attempts to dismiss this experience as beer-induced imagination or a recollection from history courses at college have not dimmed the peculiar sensation of getting caught in a timeless world of deep memory.

I can give you a dozen other examples of similar experiences that have occurred during my lifetime. I'll share another.

Tom Sugrue and I hated each other from the day we met. We didn't know how to handle this. We tried, but it was too difficult. We hurt each other psychologically and, at times, physically—fighting, bickering, causing confusion for ourselves, our roommates, and our friends. Our freshman year at Washington and Lee was practically a continuous argument, mainly about two subjects—Edgar Cayce and the Catholic Church.

Finally, he ridiculed Dad one too many times. I dared him to come home with me and meet him. That was a turning point. Dad gave him a life reading, which traced the roots of our problems to ancient Egypt. Tom fell in love with my family. And we began what became a life-long friendship.

When Tom's wife Mary went into the hospital to have their first child, Tom went in to get his knee looked at. They put him in a sweat cabinet and raised the temperature to kill the germs. Mary came out with a baby girl, but Tom came out looking like a skeleton. His arms and legs had no flesh on them—he couldn't walk. He was a horrible sight. Tom wanted to ask Dad for a reading, but Mary refused. She said the readings were not scientific, maybe the work of the devil. She finally agreed when she feared Tom might be dying.

Tom's reading said that the doctors had burned the lining of his intestinal tract, which absorbs food for the body. The reading said he was dying, but it could be prevented. It recommended Epsom salts baths, light massage, Atomidine, and the wet cell appliance. I took the appliance and everything, went to New York, stayed at Tom's for a week, and started him on the treatments. Soon Mary's father got sick, and she couldn't handle them both.

In 1939, Tom came to live at our house and stayed two years. He was very thin, and his arms and legs were stiff. Dad continued to give readings and prescribe treatments.

I did everything for Tom in those years—massaged him every day, took him out and got him in the ocean. I was running a Boy Scout troop, and they'd come by and carry him anywhere. He and I prayed, meditated, and played chess together. I really cared for him in every way and learned to care for him deeply as a soul. Dad saved Tom's life; I'm sure of it. We worked through one of the most difficult pieces of karma I've ever heard of. And we became friends at a level well beyond the average. It was beautiful.

In 1952, he went into a New York hospital for the last time. I had arranged to take time off to go see him, but the night before I was scheduled to go, I went to his hospital room in a dream. Alone in bed, he greeted me and said, "I'll be with you in a minute." His finer body then separated from his flesh body. He got up from the bed and walked with me to another room, where we sat by ourselves and talked. He said, "I'm going soon, and I'm very happy about it. I can't deal with this pain any longer. But there's no use your spending the time and money to come here to see me. I won't know you. I will hear you, but I won't consciously recognize you. I know you would come. And now you have."

Then we talked of other things and he said, "I'll continue to try to help in any way I can."

He died in January 1953 at forty-five.

I never loved another man as I loved Tom. I never hated anyone more thoroughly either, nor enjoyed hating anyone as much as I enjoyed hating Tom. I've had some very deep friendships in my life but have never known one with all the ambivalence and change of this one. I certainly never worked harder at a relationship, and neither did he. In the end, he trusted me and I trusted him, completely, and we could be absolutely frank with each other.

One final experience:

Around the early '60s, I began to feel a rage building in me. At the time I was head of this growing worldwide organization—the A.R.E., whose motto included the word *love*—and I found myself hating people if they did something I didn't like. My fellow workers, people I rubbed shoulders with every day, were making me angry, and I had no control over it. I often felt ticked off, cross. It was making me sick.

Years ago, Dad had warned me: " . . . prepare thine self. *Burn* those of desire to rule, as of old . . . " (3976-7)

He was referring to another life when I'd been a king.

I recognized that my behavior was out of line, but I couldn't correct it. I found myself planning and doing things that were not right, taking advantage of people, hurting them because I didn't like them, because I hated them. I'd get rid of them—people I worked with at the A.R.E., members, people I was dealing with every day. I could get so angry that I could destroy individuals without batting an eye, just get rid of them, turn away from them, not deal with them. It was very dangerous and successful. You play people against people. A lot of businesses are run this way. And I couldn't seem to do anything about it.

Yet, here I was, head of this wonderful, spiritual organization. I knew that if I kept on the way I was, I'd come apart, and the A.R.E. would come apart.

So I kept on praying and meditating; in fact, kept at it all the harder as I (and others) became aware of my distraught state, and I had this, I don't know, a dream or a vision, but all I could remember was a voice: "Go to Egypt!"

I didn't have any money, so I organized the first A.R.E. tour of forty-some people, and off we went to Egypt. We went up the Nile to Ramses' great temple at Abu-Simbel, into a back room where the gods were supposed to come. We asked the guards to leave and had a meditation. I said the affirmation and then began to smother.

I decided there were too many people in this little room and imagined all these ladies passing out and our having to drag them out. So I opened my eyes and looked around. They were fine. There was nothing wrong with them. It was me; I couldn't breathe. I thought I was having a heart attack. I shut my eyes and said the affirmation again.

It was like somebody snatched the floor out from under me, and I sank into another world—a book-of-life kind of thing—into another body, somebody else, a foreigner from another country, a slave with a rope around my neck, many of us roped together, a chain gang. Egyptians were walking beside me. My feet were tied in bloody rags. My hands, crossed behind me, were in pain. The Egyptian near me had a whip, a short-handled whip with leather thongs and rocks in the tips. He whipped me. I stumbled. The whip came over my shoulder and took about an inch of flesh off my chest. I cursed him in a strange language, which he apparently understood because he hit me with the butt of the whip. It pulled me down, and the others ahead of and behind me. I hated him, and that hatred was so terrible, it was like a fire inside me.

Then I was in another life, back in the time of Ramses II, on a scaffold chiseling the stone walls that our tour group had passed on the way in. The artist who had drawn these designs on the wall was completing some inlay nearby. I would chisel, and he would fill it in with gold or other precious metal. I could feel the patches of hardened skin on my knees and my hand where I'd missed with the hammer and hit myself, where it had bled and become encrusted. I had to stay there for hours at a time. It was miserable.

The overseer this time had a long staff with a lever thing on the end of it. He could reach anyone on the scaffold with it. He hit me on the back because I had made a small error in chiseling. I hated that man with such violence that it raged inside me while I experienced this.

Then I was in another life—a little boy dying in my Egyptian mother's arms. My stomach was swollen. We were starving. The Nile had not flooded, and the crops had not matured. There was nothing to eat, only water.

Finally I came to, back to meditation, back to the temple with our tour group. I knew where my anger, fear, and rage had come from.

I prayed about this very hard.

Then we went to Israel, to Galilee and Capernaum, to a village on the north coast of the Sea of Galilee. It was beautiful. The guide was showing us what they thought was Peter's house way back in the time of Jesus.

I turned away and walked down to the water. There was a wall—beyond it grass and trees. It was so beautiful. As I stood there, drinking in this scene, a light formed—taller than I, and oval. It moved over to encompass me, until I was enclosed in this otherworldly light. It was the greatest peace I've ever felt. I was so joyous. I asked in my mind if I could go get Sally and share it with her, and I knew I could.

So I ran and got her, pulled her away from the group, and walked with her down to the Sea of Galilee, and stood in that same place. The light enveloped us both, and I was healed.

Since then I've had far, far better control over my fears and angers and hates.

The concept of rebirth then, for me, is not merely a concept. It is a fact of life which raises crucial questions about the meaning of life and death.

20

Suggestions for the Living

Dreams

What can you do if you decide you don't want to wait until you die to experience this inner world? Or, if you've already experienced it, what can you do to heighten and lighten your experience? You can begin by studying your dreams.

Invariably, when I've suggested this, people make excuses and look for ways to avoid it. They say their dreams are too crazy, mixed-up, grotesque, or revealing. They say they couldn't possibly find anything beneficial in their particular hodgepodge of images. They claim support from therapists, who insist we need help to understand dreams.

However, the Talmud says that unremembered dreams are like unopened letters. Cayce, in over a thousand readings on dreams and dream interpretations, said that nothing of importance ever happens to us that isn't first previewed in a dream. He also declared that dreams contain all kinds of usually unnoticed psychic phenomena—telepathy, communication with the dead, clairvoyance, past-life recall. In my experience, the very act of dreaming and remembering my dreams has been healing, renewing, and revitalizing.

Cayce outlined three general types of dreams: (1) those from the conscious mind, the senses, such as a hard spot in the bed or a barking dog; (2) those from the subconscious mind, where the acts of the previous day are compared with our desires, attitudes, and ideals; and (3) those from the superconscious mind, which can be "visionary."

When you first start studying your dreams, it's like learning a foreign language. Before you can understand what they're saying, you must learn single words, then phrases, and finally sentences. In the same way, it's not possible to understand your dreams without first learning their language. To do this, you must begin writing them down and studying them. This is a sure, sound, and safe way to explore your unconscious mind.

Place a notebook, pad, and pencil near your bed where you can reach them while you're half-awake. When you write, don't try to describe whole scenes, just jot down key words—nouns or verbs. You can fill in the rest in the morning.

As you drift off to sleep, repeat to yourself, "I will remember my dreams." This is very important. It impresses your subconscious, lets it know you're serious.

Don't be discouraged if it doesn't work the first time. Keep at it. Persistence will eventually produce results. Desire, will, and practice—the same factors that work with any skill—can help you become acquainted with the most exciting dimensions of your real self—the self we all inhabit when we pass through God's Other Door.

If you decide you want to study the subject in more depth, there are many good books on dreams and dreaming.

Prayer

What can you do if you've already experienced this inner world, but want to heighten and lighten your experience? What can you do if you decide you want to experience God's Light?

In 1923, when I was sixteen, after Cayce suggested that we'd all benefit from dream study, I began recording mine. Certain symbols recurred, in particular a disreputable character who smoked, drank, leered, and winked slyly. Since he looked very much like an unkempt me, I took him to be a symbol of my lower self. One night I met him leaning against a lamppost on a dim street. As I came opposite him, he threw away his cigarette and tackled me around the knees. We both rolled into the gutter. Gradually, I grew afraid of him. Shortly after this I faced perplexing temptations.

In my dreams, he continued to get me into a variety of difficulties. Finally, not knowing what else to do, I began praying for him. In a later dream, he complained bitterly that I was taking unfair advantage. Nevertheless, prayer made my life easier.

In a reading on November 19, 1932, at Virginia Beach, Edgar Cayce defined prayer:

. . . prayer is the *making* of one's conscious self

more in attune with the spiritual forces that may
manifest in a material world . . .

[Prayer is] the pouring out of the personality of
the individual, or a group who enter in for the purpose of either outward show to be seen by men; or
that enter in even as in the closet of one's inner self
and pours out self that the inner man may be filled
with the Spirit of the Father in His merciful kindness to men . . .

Prayer is the concerted effort of the physical consciousness to become attuned to the consciousness
of the Creator, either collectively or individually!
281-13

Four types of prayer are generally recognized—con-
fession, thanksgiving, adoration, and petition.

Meditation

Years ago, about a month after I began meditating, I
had a strange and beautiful experience. It was spring. I
was seated looking east from the third floor of an ocean-
front home at Virginia Beach. After the initial procedures, an almost painful stillness came over me, then an
incredible humming in my head, like the sound you
might hear if you placed your ear against a high-tension
tower. Then came the most beautiful music I've ever
heard. I have no words to describe that music. Over the
intervening years, though diligent about meditating, I've
never heard that music again. It may happen, though,
tomorrow, or the next day. I keep meditating; I keep hop-
ing.

Meditation is different from prayer. This is how Cayce
defined it in a reading given on June 20, 1944, at Virginia
Beach, for a woman, forty-nine:

Prayer is supplication to God and meditation is listening to His answer. 2946-6

In a reading on July 20, 1944, at Virginia Beach, for a salesman, twenty-nine, this was given:

Then set definite periods for prayer; set definite periods for meditation. Know the difference between each. Prayer, in short, is appealing to the divine within self, the divine from without self, and meditation is keeping still in body, in mind, in heart, listening, listening to the voice of thy Maker. 5368-1

On November 19, 1932, at Virginia Beach for the Glad Helpers Prayer Group, these distinctions were made:

Meditation, then, is prayer, but is prayer from *within* the *inner* self, and partakes not only of the physical inner man but the soul that is aroused by the spirit of man from within.
... there are *definite* conditions that arise from within the inner man when an individual enters into true or deep meditation. A physical condition happens, a physical activity takes place! Acting through what? Through that man has chosen to call the imaginative or the impulsive, and the sources of impulse are aroused by the shutting out of thought pertaining to activities or attributes of the carnal forces of man.
... *Meditation* is [the] *emptying* self of all that hinders the creative forces from rising along the natural channels of the physical man to be disseminated through those centers and sources that create the activities of the physical, the mental, the

spiritual man; properly done must make one *stronger* mentally, physically . . . 281-13

Forty participants at the eighth A.R.E. Congress on June
15, 1939, at the Warner Hotel, Virginia Beach, were told:

[Meditation] is the attuning of the mental body
and the physical body to its spiritual source. 281-41

In a reading on April 21, 1932, at Virginia Beach for the
Glad Helpers Prayer Group, I asked:

(Q) . . . How can I develop greater spiritual control over the mental body during meditation?
(A) The more that there is held that the mental
and physical body is surrounded by, is protected by,
that consciousness of the Master that gave, "I will
not leave thee comfortless," and the greater the
physical can be submerged, the greater will be the
activity of the spiritual forces in and through such
bodies.
(Q) Please interpret for us what is meant by the
symbols, the rod and cup?
(A) *All* must pass under the rod as of that *cleansing* necessary for the inflowing of the Christ Consciousness, even as *He* passed under the rod,
partook of the cup—and *gives* same to others.
281-5

In a reading on April 27, 1934, at Norfolk, Virginia, for
the Glad Helpers Prayer Group, a travel agent, thirty-one,
[603], asked how to improve her healing meditation. She
was told:

Not so much self-development, but rather devel-

oping the Christ Consciousness in self, being self-
less, that He may have *His* way with thee, that He—
the Christ—may direct thy ways, that He will guide
thee in the things thou doest, thou sayest. 281-20

In a reading on April 28, 1936, at the David Kahn home
in New York City, the following was given to a woman
student, twenty-two:

Meditate upon those activities that may be
motivat[ed] by the desires of the *inner* self, rather
than the glorification of the material self. 1189-1

In a reading on April 17, 1944, at Virginia Beach, a
music teacher, thirty-eight, received counsel about
meditation:

There is much more in anticipation and hope
and desire than in being satisfied or gratified. Always know that there is more, if the whole trust is in
the Lord. 1861-18

Meditation is a way of preparing for the afterlife.
In a reading on November 2, 1937, at Virginia Beach, a
housewife, forty-nine, Christian, was told:

Yet in the deeper meditations, in those experiences when those influences may arise when the
spirit of the Creative Force, the universality of soul,
of mind—not as material, not as judgments, not *in*
time and space but *of* time and space—may become lost in the Whole, instead of the entity being
lost in the maze of confusing influences—then the
soul visions arise in the meditations. 987-4

Pray for yourself and others after every meditation.
The advantages of this will become apparent later.

Gradually there will come a quieting of the body. The
conscious mind will grow still. Pictures and scenes from
the subconscious will stop flickering. At this point you
may be ready to begin deeper meditation. Longer periods will be possible and rewarding. Finally, you will
reach a point of stillness. At this point, there will be light.
For some it will be a tiny point of brilliant white light.
For others it may be a golden speck or a tiny ball. For
others it may be a warm and penetrating flow of light.
Consciousness, at this point, can be moved to the light.

Service

Thousands of times during forty-three years of readings, Cayce stressed the need for service. As a family
man, a member of church, community, city, and nation,
Dad tried daily to put that precept into action. Here's
some advice he gave for himself:

The *consciousness* of the ability to serve is only by
service, not by just wishing. But how has it been
given? Desire of such a nature as to act, as to will,
and act with the fusion of will and desire towards
that purpose! *Fear* being cast aside by the very abilities of the self-submerging of the physical consciousness through those influences as has so oft
been indicated, makes for an attunement to those
sources sought by the individual seeker. 294-185

In a reading on April 28, 1936, at the David Kahn home
in NewYork City, a woman student, twenty-two, was urged:

Become, then, a channel of blessings to others,
and thus may the beauties of the *heavenly* forces—

as may be expressed in such—be thine very own.
Beauty for Beauty's sake. Love that it may be the
manifestations of not bodily emotions, but rather
those that show forth *His* activity in and among
men. 1189-1

In a reading on October 18, 1932, at Virginia Beach, a
housewife, thirty-one, Protestant, asked if her husband
were to blame for her depression:

This is rather from within self, but losing self in
aid for others—and in doing that which gives joy to
the inner self will relieve much of these. 1928-1

In a reading on May 26, 1944, at Virginia Beach, a
woman, fifty-eight, who asked how to overcome fear of
old age and being alone, was told:

By going out and doing something for somebody
else; that is, those not able to do for themselves,
making others happy, forgetting self entirely. These
are as material manifestations but in helping someone else you'll get rid of your feelings [of fear].
5226-1

In a mental and spiritual reading on February 8, 1941,
at Virginia Beach, Minnie Barrett asked:

(Q) How may I overcome the innate doubt or fear
which prevents attunement with the Christ, as
promised?
(A) Just keeping on keeping on in the trust—
trust—in Him! No *direct* way may be experienced
for self by another—and yet the entity finds self very
oft close to being directed in that way. Hold fast to

Him! Let that which causes doubt or fear be taken up in the willingness, the desire, to be of help to others. 69-4

In a reading on May 13, 1942, at Virginia Beach, for the Glad Helpers Prayer Group, Hannah Miller was counseled:

Let fear, let worry, be lost in thy service to others for His name's sake. Let thy heart be lifted up, that ye may hear that "Well done" from Him, who is mindful of those who seek His face. 281-61

In a reading on February 20, 1944, for a woman, twenty-nine, who had had twenty-seven different jobs, was wondering about her life's purpose, and had heard of Cayce through *Coronet* magazine, Edgar Cayce said:

First be conscious of this—that the Lord hath need of thee with thy faults, with thy virtues. For without the consciousness that thou art His and He is thine, ye may not claim that birthright, ye may not pass this way without sorrow or without condemnation. But with that consciousness He healeth thy diseases, He instructeth thy mind, He pointeth the way that ye will choose. 3685-1

In a reading on August 17, 1943, at Virginia Beach, a woman, sixty-six, who'd heard of Edgar Cayce through *There Is a River*, was told:

Know it is in the little things, not by thunderous applause, not by the ringing of bells, nor the blowing of whistles, that the Son of Man comes— humble, gently, kind, meek, lowly—for "He that is the greatest among you serveth all." 3161-1

21

Light

Jesus said in John 8:12: "I am the light of the world,"
and, before the Last Supper, in John 12:35-36: "Yet a little
while is the light with you. Walk while ye have the light,
lest darkness come upon you: for he that walketh in darkness knoweth not whither he goeth. While ye have light,
believe in the light, that ye may be the children of light."

The sleeping Cayce also made many references to light:

In a reading on May 27, 1944, at Virginia Beach, for a
woman, twenty-six, teacher, social worker, Presbyterian,
it was stated:

> ... God moved and said, "Let there be light," and
> there was light, not the light of the sun, but rather

that of which, through which, in which every soul had, has, and ever has its being. 5246-1

In a reading on November 1, 1936, for the Search for God Study Group, Norfolk #1, Cayce gave this affirmation:

Our Father, our God, may the light of Thy wisdom, of Thy strength, of Thy power, guide—as we would apply ourselves in Thy service for others. In His name we seek. 262-102

This was given in a reading on March 15, 1939, at Virginia Beach for the Glad Helpers Prayer Group:

O God of mercy and light! 281-40

In a reading on December 30, 1937, at Virginia Beach, for a housewife, forty-eight, Protestant, this was presented in a prayer:

Father-Mother God, here am I—Thy handmaid! Weak, unworthy though I may be—I come seeking Divine light . . . 1504-1

In a reading on May 22, 1935, at Virginia Beach, a woman, seventy-six, sought interpretation of a tiny light that often came into her vision. It would vibrate rapidly, then gradually form a near circle with very brilliant lights zigzagging. This would last for fifteen minutes; then she would have a headache for six hours. It came upon her suddenly, during the night or day, sometimes twice a day. At first it came months apart, but now occurred frequently. She wanted to know what to do. Edgar Cayce advised:

... the elimination of this should not be sought; for the body has builded in its *mental* self that reaction which recurs.

So, rather understand and comprehend same from a spiritual angle. And when such conditions begin, *enter* rather into spiritual attunement with the mental forces than attempting to vision the phenomenon as it appears ...

Thus, as we will find, we will come to see not only the light but—by the deep meditation—may enter in and become a portion *of* the light, that may bring helpful *healing* attributes *to* the psychological conditions in the body.

Hence, guard self by the *Infinite*. Or when there are those reactions, enter in—using this affirmation:

Let no influence, Father, be within this experience that does not bespeak of Thy glory to Thy children. Let the light of Thy countenance be only that as may come to me now. Through the promises Thou hast made do I claim, do I seek, do I ask, Thy protection. 774-3

In closing I'm going to tell of a personal experience with the Light.

For, as death is a birth into another experience, so also with birth. We die there, we're born here. It is a door; another of God's doors.

Edgar Cayce put it this way in a reading for himself and Morton Blumenthal on March 17, 1927, at Virginia Beach:

Yet, as we find, there is in all the world nothing that offers so much possibility as when the body of the human is born into the material plane. 5756-4

We have two boys, you know. When Sally became pregnant the first time, Dr. Wally Taylor, Sally's brother, told us it would be a difficult birth. He sent her to a specialist, and the specialist said it would be a difficult birth. We got a reading from Edgar Cayce, and he said it would be a difficult birth. So we followed the reading, and we followed the specialist's directions, and we did all that her brother told her to do, and all that the readings said to do. And we prayed.

In spite of all that, when the birth happened, it went on for hours and hours. It was pretty rough. Sally almost died, and the child almost died. (He didn't, though, he's around—Charles Thomas.)

The war came, and I went overseas, and Dad died, and Mother died, and I came back and Sally wanted another child. And I did, too.

We prayed about it and prayed about it. She was willing to try again, to go through that horrible experience. It could happen again, or it could be easy, they said. But there was still the problem, the danger.

Dad was gone—we couldn't get a reading. But we did everything the first reading said. We got another specialist—the first one had died. Her doctor brother was still there to advise us. We prepared for this second child. Lots of praying again. But as the time came closer, I became more disturbed and worried.

I came in one night from a lecture, and went into her room, and sat down on the edge of the bed. She was asleep. And I prayed.

I was awake. I was more awake than I usually am, though you can believe I was asleep, if it'll help you accept what I'm about to say. As I prayed, a Light went on— a brilliant white Light in the corner of the room. It was a little room, and it filled that whole corner. And in it were my mother's face, and my father's face, and they were alive, full of energy and vitality. Dad spoke to me—not in words, but in my head. He smiled and said, "Hugh Lynn, you should not worry, you shouldn't be concerned. It's going to be all right. We are going to show you what Love can do."

He smiled, and Mother smiled, and they moved. They moved in this Light, and as it touched me, I lost consciousness as I know consciousness. I lost it completely. But I became aware of my father, and my mother, and of their essence, and my essence. And we were all together in what I'd call an ecstasy, a state of tremendous emotion, beauty, an ecstasy—however you want to spell it. There isn't but one word for it. We haven't any language, except the language of love that even comes close to this. Then we moved—all three of us with the Light into Sally's body and the body of this unborn child. The ecstasy increased until it was overpowering, and it swept over me like waves rolling over top. I couldn't stand it—I mean there was nothing left of me. I was out of my body—I was in this other body. And the Life was there in the body of this child—the essence—all five of us together, and it was like being all together.

Then there was a pull, and we moved out of Sally's body, and I was on the bed again, and the Light was in the corner, and Dad and Mother were there.

I was crying, choked. I couldn't talk. I couldn't say anything. Dad grinned at me. He didn't smile, he grinned, a big, wide grin. And he said, "You see? You see what Love can do?"

Mother smiled and said, "It's gonna be all right. It's gonna be a boy, and it's gonna be all right."

Then the Light went out, and I sat there, sobbing.

Sally woke up, turned over, grabbed hold of my hand, and squeezed it very hard. Before I could say a word, she said, "Hugh Lynn, it's gonna be all right. I've had a beautiful dream of your mother and father. We're going to have a son. It's gonna be all right."

And it was. The birth was exceedingly easy. We hardly made it to the hospital. The specialist didn't get there. Her brother didn't get there. She was delivered by an intern. It was a very easy birth.

So, when some of you ask, do I think I've had contact with Edgar Cayce, you know what my answer is.

There is another plane of consciousness. And love, more than anything else, bridges this distance, just as it bridges the horrible distances right here on earth that we sometimes put between each other.

22

The Continuity of Life

[This lecture by Edgar Cayce was given in February 1934.]

First, let us understand what we mean by certain terms that we must use. Not being a scientist, I cannot speak in a scientific way and manner. I am not an educated man, so I cannot speak in terms of a scholar. I can speak only from experience and observation, or from what I have read.

When we use the term "continuity of life," what do we mean by "life"? Do we mean that span from birth until death? Would it not be preferable to refer to life as the consciousness of existence?

With such a premise, I approach this question which has been sounded throughout the ages. It is one of the oldest questions that man has considered. If a man die, shall he live again? What is death? What comes next? All of these sound the same note. We must each answer within our own self. But this is my belief:

I believe that when God breathed into man the breath of life he became a LIVING SOUL—individual soul, if you please. The Spirit of God is life, whether in a blade of grass or in man! The soul of man is individual and lives on!

In the very first part of the Bible we find it noted that man was forbidden to partake of certain fruit in the Garden. In the partaking of that fruit he became conscious of his being, and it was sin—for he was forbidden to do it.

Then God reasoned with man that he must leave the Garden lest he partake of the tree of life and live forever. What did that mean? Just that? Or had Satan been correct when he said, "Ye shall not surely die if ye partake of this fruit"? What brought physical death to man? Error! The partaking of that which he was forbidden. Did it bring death to the soul? No! It brought death to the physical body!

Not to become conscious of our continued existence is to become righteous in ourselves. Then we may become conscious of our continued existence, whether in the physical realm, the spiritual realm, or whatever stage of development through which we may be passing from physical life unto spiritual life. As we pass through all the various stages, what are we attempting to gain? Righteousness within!

Jesus gave that if we had His consciousness within us we should become conscious, or should *know* what He has said to us from the beginning. What was the beginning with Christ? "In the beginning was the Word, and the Word was with God, and the Word was God." So were our souls in the beginning. The Master said, "Ye say that ye have Abraham for your father. I say unto you that be-

fore Abraham was I AM, and he rejoiced to see my day
and he saw it and was glad!" Then many of those to
whom He spoke these words walked no longer with Him,
but turned away. Why? He was answering that same
question which has been bothering man from the beginning: "If a man die, will he live again?" He said to
Nicodemus, "Know ye not that a man must be born
again?" When Nicodemus asked, "How can such things
be?" He answered, "Are ye a teacher in Israel and knoweth
not these things?"

What is it to know the continuity of life? It is to be righteous within, and to have the consciousness of the Christ
within. For God is Life. Christ is Life, and Light unto all
that seek to know Him; and without Him—is there any
other way? *Is* there any other way? Not that He is the *only*
way, but "He that climbeth up some other way is a thief
and a robber" to his own self! He *is* the Life. He came to
represent that life, and the continuity of life is in the immortality of the soul.

Immortality of the soul is an *individual* thing. My soul
is my own, with the ability to know itself to be itself, and
yet *one with God.* That was the message Jesus gave to His
disciples all the way through. "I of myself can do nothing," but the Life that is within—and the gift of God
working in you—will make *you* conscious of *your* relationship to your Maker. How do we become conscious
of our relationship with God? By living the Fruits of the
Spirit! Spirit is the Life, and Light, that makes us conscious of immortality—which is the continuation of our
oneness with god. If God *is* Life, we then must *be His* to
enjoy the consciousness of being one with Him!

Continuity of Life, then, is being conscious of our oneness with God, through the channel that has been set
before us by the Example that has come into the world
to show us the Way of Life.

That consciousness exists after physical death has very clearly been pointed out to us in at least two ways that I should like to mention.

After Samuel passed on, Saul was still in trouble. He knew Samuel had rebuked him for the manner of life he had lived, yet he was in great distress and sought to know if Samuel would not give him another blessing—though Samuel had passed from the physical plane of existence. So Saul sought out a channel through whom he might speak to Samuel—and spoke to him! We find that Samuel's consciousness had not changed one iota by having passed to the other side, for his first words to Saul were along the same lines that he used while still on earth, "Why troublest thou me? Dost thou not know God has rejected thee already?"

Passing over did not automatically make Samuel know more than he knew when he was here; not a bit more; the manner of existence he had lived in this plane had only developed him just so far. What did Christ say about this? "As the tree falls, so shall it lie!" When we pass into another plane, our development *begins* right there in that plane. Just as our birth into the physical brings a gradual unfoldment and development in the physical.

Therefore I believe there is a gradual growth throughout. What is Truth? Growth! What is Life? God! The knowledge of God, then, is the growth into Life—or the *continuity of Life itself!*

We have another example of continuity pointed out to us in the parable which Christ gave of the rich man and Lazarus. They had both passed into what we call the death state, yet both were conscious. Living, then, is being conscious of your experience—or conscious of where you are!

Dives, the rich man, lifted his eyes, for he was in torment. Why was he in torment? Where was torment? What is torment? We want to have these questions answered in our own consciousness in our own figure of speech, so that we can encompass what we are talking about. We want to give things metes and bounds. We want to tag them with names, and, even so, we may not recognize them the next time someone calls those names. We have gotten names for almost everything, yet when we say a name, it even now means an entirely different thing to each one of us. It is our experience with that named which makes the difference; it is our own development. The same word may have varied meanings.

The place Dives occupied was his own building, his own development—and he was being tormented in a flame. Tormented in a flame of what? Fire? Well, he had the consciousness that it was fire, so it must have been something like it—for he wanted water to put it out!

It was a continued existence for that man, and he saw Lazarus in Abraham's bosom. He recognized Abraham, though he had never seen him. How? He recognized Lazarus, though possibly he had never paid any attention to him while on earth. How? You answer it. But he *was conscious* of the condition. He was *conscious!*

Most of us believe the Scripture; at least we believe what is written there is for our knowledge and our understanding. And if we follow that, we will come to a greater knowledge of Life—that is, God. We will come to a greater concept of how great Life is.

I would like to go into the subject of just how consciousness has to do with life and death—but that is reincarnation. Why are we not conscious of the continuity of life in the physical plane? Why do we not remember when we live again? We do not remember because we have not been righteous enough! Christ said that if we had His consciousness within us He would bring to our remembrance all things from the very beginning!

It once bothered me a great deal as a child that God spoke to the people in the Bible and did not speak to us. Now I believe that He does and will speak to us if we will only listen. So often we allow the desires of our physical bodies to so outweigh our desires for spiritual knowledge that we build barriers between ourselves and God. *We do it ourselves,* for "He is the same yesterday, today, and forever," and He does not *will* that any should be lost. What prevents us from knowing more about Life, or God? Ourselves! Nothing can separate us from the love of God but ourselves—nothing! It is the will of man that can make him conscious of the knowledge of God and of all Life; it is the will of man that can separate him from God—because he enjoys rather the pleasures of the flesh for a season. "I will satisfy the desires of my body now, rather than listen to the voice that may be raised within."

I choose to think that each one of us has an individual soul, that there is *One* Spirit—the Spirit of God—going through each and every one, that makes each and every one of us akin—that makes all life and all nature akin; for Life in *every* form is dependent upon that force we call God. For, as matter came into being, it was permeated with the Spirit of God that gives life, with its ability to *carry itself on* and *make of itself* that which has been determined by God that it should be. Man only, who was chosen to be one with God—and a companion with Him from the beginning, chose rather to go his own way—as Adam. But He has prepared a way, through the Christ, who came into the world that we through Him might have life and have it more abundantly; that we at all periods of our development might be more conscious of the life of God that is within us. Christ Himself taught that we must test the spirits, and those who acknowledge that Jesus the Christ has come in the flesh are born of God. The Truth makes alive, and the Life makes you free.

Don't ever think that your life isn't being written in the Book of Life! I found it! I have seen it! It is being written; *YOU are the writer!* As to how close it is going to be to your Savior and to your God, you alone can answer. You alone! It is our own soul development. It is up to us to answer.

If we would have life, if we would reach that Promised Land, if we would reach that consciousness, if we would become aware of our relationship, we must *live it here and now*—and then the next step is given to us. That has been His promise, and His promises are sure.

A.R.E. PRESS

The A.R.E. Press publishes books, videos, and audiotapes meant to improve the quality of our readers' lives—personally, professionally, and spiritually. We hope our products support your endeavors to realize your career potential, to enhance your relationships, to improve your health, and to encourage you to make the changes necessary to live a loving, joyful, and fulfilling life.

For more information or to receive a free catalog, call:

1-800-723-1112

Or write:

A.R.E. Press
215 67th Street
Virginia Beach, VA 23451-2061

Discover How the Edgar Cayce Material Can Help You!

The Association for Research and Enlightenment, Inc. (A.R.E.®), was founded in 1931 by Edgar Cayce. Its international headquarters are in Virginia Beach, Virginia, where thousands of visitors come year-round. Many more are helped and inspired by A.R.E.'s local activities in their own hometowns or by contact via mail (and now the Internet!) with A.R.E. headquarters.

People from all walks of life, all around the world, have discovered meaningful and life-transforming insights in the A.R.E. programs and materials, which focus on such areas as personal spirituality, holistic health, dreams, family life, finding your best vocation, reincarnation, ESP, meditation, and soul growth in small-group settings. Call us today at our toll-free number:

1-800-333-4499

or

Explore our electronic visitors center on the
Internet: **http://www.edgarcayce.org**

We'll be happy to tell you more about how the work of the A.R.E. can help you!

A.R.E.
215 67th Street
Virginia Beach, VA 23451-2061